ROBERT SMITH'S
YOUNG SHOWJUMPER

ROBERT SMITH'S
YOUNG SHOWJUMPER

Selecting • Training • Competing

RACHEL LAMBERT

with additional material by Anne Plume

Photographs by BOB LANGRISH

David & Charles

Page 2
Hickstead 1990:
Robert successfully negotiates the Derby Bank with Silver Dust

British Library Cataloguing-in-Publication Data

Lambert, Rachel
    Robert Smith's young showjumper: selecting,
    training, competing.
    I. Title
    798.2

ISBN 0-7153-9921-7

Printed in Italy
by New Interlitho SpA, Milan
for David & Charles
Brunel House   Newton Abbot   Devon

Contents

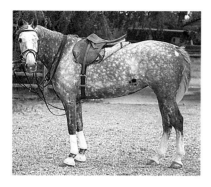

Robert Smith is the younger son of that great showjumping personality Harvey Smith, and by hard work and persistence has managed to follow in his father's footsteps with remarkable success. However, he is the first to admit that the early 'pony days' were quite a struggle – in fact for Robert and younger brother Steven those all-important first experiences in the saddle were on donkeys rather than ponies, because their father felt 'donkey power' provided a much more reliable way for a small child to gain confidence initially. So it was on a donkey called Jerusalem that three-year-old Robert learnt the rudiments of riding at his family's home in Shipley, West Yorkshire. Moreover right from the start of their equestrian career, Harvey was never prepared to indulge his sons with expensive ponies; the successes they enjoyed as juniors were entirely due to the hard work and dedication put in by the boys themselves. In particular Robert recalls the fun that he and Steven had with two little greys called Bill and Ben; learning to stick on when they bucked and were naughty, jumping round the local gymkhanas, these ponies taught both boys basic riding skills which stood them in good stead for the rest of their lives. Robert and Steven's mother was a terrific support when they were youngsters: taking them to shows, giving them general help and guidance; in the same way as did Mrs Whitaker, mother of the famous showjumping brothers John and Michael. She would also help exercise the horses, although she was not, herself, a keen competitor; she preferred to let the rest of her family take the limelight. Because Harvey was always busy competing himself he had very little free time, and was therefore unable to advise and help his sons with their jumping technique to any great extent. Nor were the boys ever members of the Pony Club, or any other riding club for that

Introduction

Robert stresses the importance
of having someone on the
ground to give advice to the
rider. It is not always easy to
accept criticism, but a self-
criticial rider will certainly
progress. There is no room for
complacency where horses are
concerned!

i
n
t
r
o
d
u
c
t
i
o
n

matter. However, if there *were* occasions when expert help was required, they knew their father would always spare them an hour or so when he could, and offer his advice to try and help sort out any problems. Many experienced trainers and riders feel that Harvey can get the best out of even the most difficult horses – nowadays his skills are sought by racehorse trainers, to improve the jumping technique of their National Hunt horses – so his knowledge and experience, when he had time to give it, was invaluable to both Robert and Steven. Nonetheless, the boys often found they were left to climb their way up the ladder the hard way.

Robert has come a long way since his first show: this great event took place when he was nine years old on a pony called Blackboy, and it was the first of many, all helping to lay the foundations of experience – and some of them giving him a foretaste of that 'spectator opinion' which so often seemed to accompany the Smith family. Even in those early days Robert suffered a certain spectator animosity: it was assumed that any son of Harvey Smith would be provided with expensive ponies, so if he won a competition, onlookers immediately attributed his success to 'Harvey's influence'; and if he lost, he was quite simply considered 'useless'. This form of 'labelling' had a considerable influence on Robert's outlook, and from an early stage in his career he set out to prove that it was his own skill and ability to ride a horse, and not his father's influence, which brought him success. With typical Yorkshire determination he has proved beyond dispute that the remarkable progress he has made, and the many wins he has enjoyed since that first show with Blackboy, are due to his talent as a rider and horseman.

As a boy, Robert had serious aspirations to become a boxer, but showjumping soon took precedence and it wasn't too long before boxing gloves were forfeited for riding gloves – and from then onwards there was no doubt as to where his loyalties lay. He rode more and more during his early teens under the expert guidance of his father's farrier, Harvey Kay – but otherwise he is the first to confess that he has never received any 'real' riding lessons in his life! However, in response to Robert's enthusiasm and dedication, Harvey Kay helped him with the groundwork and basic training so essential to the career of any showjumper, and

A good rider has to be a perfectionist

this education was invaluable. Harvey Kay was also responsible for the early training of Peter Murphy, Alan Fazakerley, Mark Fuller, Michael Mac and many other talented young riders.

Robert's natural talent as a horseman is widely recognised by his fellow riders, who feel that he has never had the class of horse he deserves. His skill and ability were in part instilled by the many difficult ponies that 'taught him to sit properly in the saddle and learn the hard way'. But, like his father, he managed to get the best out of these very 'average' ponies, and they brought him successes which took him to the top of the junior ladder.

> I had a chestnut pony called Lovely (not the most apt of names!) and she taught me quite a bit about riding! In the arena, when I passed the entrance, she used to rear up. Another of her habits was to refuse just half a stride from a jump – so she really taught me to use my seat and legs. Another pony that helped me to develop a secure seat was a 13.2hh gelding called Collier: it was nine months before I could even stay on that pony!

Amongst other 'characters' that Robert recalls was Little Boots, a 14.2hh gelding who had an enormous kickbuck, something he used to do between fences – any lapse in concentration and Robert would be bucked off.

And then there was Mr Punch, a great little jumper, also 14.2hh but rather more stocky; many a time Robert found himself rushing past fences rather than over them, when Mr Punch's strength proved the better. Later, a horse called Speak Easy, which his father passed on to him, was a particularly unusual ride: the Smiths nick-named him 'Swizzle' because in the arena this is just what he would do, swizzle round for no apparent reason:

> I had to learn to 'out-smart' these characters, which I think is the secret of riding most horses. We can't dominate horses and ponies physically, but it *is* possible for us to get mental co-operation. However, despite the experience I undoubtedly gained from riding difficult ponies, I must stress that it is important for children and inexperienced adult riders to start on schoolmasters to give them confidence. On no account should a nervous or inexperienced rider even *consider* breaking and training a spirited young horse or pony.

Robert was always ready to learn from other riders, particularly those he most admired: Gert Wiltfang and Alwin Schockemöhle were two of the best in the seventies. That Robert himself possessed a natural aptitude for showjumping was clearly demonstrated when at just fourteen years old he was selected to compete in his first national competition, in the company of some of the world's best showjumpers. This was at the Great Yorkshire Show in 1975, on a horse called Trueman. But for Robert, the competition which at this period in his life he recalls as bringing the greatest pleasure was the Grand Prix on his home territory at the Great Yorkshire Show, which he won with a horse called Royal Rufus when he was sixteen years old:

> The course was huge at the Great Yorkshire Show, and there were about eighty competitors in the class. Winning the Grand Prix was so special because it was a great feeling when everything just seemed to click, giving me a really good buzz. I'll never forget that day!

Riding Royal Rufus, Robert was a member of the British team on the international circuit on many occasions. One of his greatest achievements was to help the team

'Fine-tuning' work at home is very important

to a gold medal in Geneva, where he himself took the bronze individual award. In 1979, on the home circuit at just seventeen years of age, Robert won the prestigious King George V Cup at the Royal International Horse Show (beating his father!) with Sanyo Video; he went on to win the title of Leading Show-jumper of the Year, and also took part in several Nations Cup competitions. Other Grade A horses with which Robert enjoyed numerous success were Merlin, Johnny Walker, Santos and Volvo, to mention but a few.

Another of Robert's more famous horses was Boysie: the bay was formerly the mount of David Bowen, and joined the yard at Shipley in 1987. Boysie was by ET Palimos out of a German mare and helped Robert to further successes, including another win in the King George V Cup in 1988, and winning the Dubai Cup at Hickstead the following year. 'Boysie was a very difficult horse to ride. He was about 15 when I had him – an old Grade A that had picked up a few bad habits. He jumped very square in front and needed to be "kept off" his fences all the time.' Since then, Robert has enjoyed many wins on different horses, among them Silver Dust, Clover and Vanessa.

The costs involved in running a team of Grade A showjumpers are phenomenal; add to this a yard full of young horses coming on, and it will soon be appreciated that to compete full-time and run a busy yard is impossible nowadays without a sponsor. Robert is the first to recognise that sponsorship from Sanyo, and then from Brook Street, has undoubtedly helped him climb to the top of the showjumping ladder – but he is never complacent about the future:

It is a difficult task finding the horsepower capable of competing at Grade A level, but is even harder staying at the top of the ladder. There are many competent Grade B horses around in Britain but many of them will never have the ability to compete at Grade A standard. Horses, like cars, need fine tuning and they will never win unless they are running smoothly – it is up to the rider to find the right balance to get the horse going well.

Nevertheless, after many years of dedicated hard work, Robert Smith was well established in the top ranks of the showjumping world. And with his own interests and commitments expanding all the time, he finally decided it was time to move from Shipley and set up on his own. In 1988 Robert moved from Yorkshire to establish his own yard at Quendon in Essex; soon after he married Leanne, and the couple continue to live at Quendon. From here he competes as much as he can, and also runs a most successful business buying and selling horses. The yard may have anything between seven and twenty-five horses, and although some of these may never make Grade As, they are highly suitable for riders who wish to compete at a slightly lower level. And of course there are the select few which *will* reach Grade A standard.

This book explains how Robert selects the young showjumping horse and how he undertakes its training, with the emphasis being on sound schooling at home. Furthermore behind every successful stable is an efficient stable management routine to keep the horses in tip-top condition: there is therefore sound advice given on this subject. The training as explained here includes taking the youngster to its first competition. Robert, like most successful horsemen, strongly believes that problems should be anticipated and prevented so that they never occur in the first place, rather than the rider struggling to correct them once they have happened. His consistently successful record goes to show how reliable this formula must be.

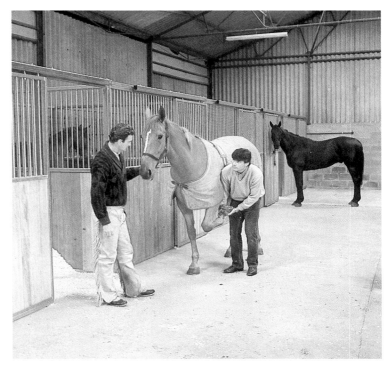

The foundations of Robert's consistent success by and large lie in a well-ordered system of stable management: the happier and healthier the horse is, the better its chances of success in competition

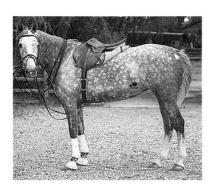

1
SELECTING

It is obviously much more difficult to judge a horse's ability when it is three or four years old than it is to assess the potential of, say, an eight-year-old which may already have started to prove itself in the showjumping arena. Everyone is searching for the perfect horse, but ultimately, 'perfection lies in the eye of the beholder' and it is the horse and rider partnership that counts. A horse may be capable of winning and being the best in the world with a rider it responds to – but with someone less compatible, who maybe fails to establish any sort of understanding with the horse, its performance can change quite dramatically. The classic example of a partnership must be John Whitaker and Milton – though admittedly there are not many horses of Milton's calibre around!

Other successful combinations include Nick Skelton and Phoenix Park, and Pierre Durand and the highly volatile Jappeloup. Phoenix Park is owned by David Broome, but despite David being an absolutely top-class rider – his successes speak for themselves – he cannot 'get a tune' out of this particular horse. But Nick Skelton and Phoenix Park just seem to 'click'. Likewise, few riders relished the idea of coping with the outstanding little Jappeloup, but through much hard work and patience on Pierre Durand's part, they emerged Olympic champions. A certain style of riding and attitude makes all the difference: the competition at the World Equestrian Games, when riders compete on each other's horses, proves this point. Top-class horses and riders can look like novices, because the rapport between horse and rider is frequently missing.

The right type

Type – as opposed to breed – is quite important when buying a horse for a certain purpose. Each equestrian discipline requires different qualities in a horse – speed for racing, stamina for endurance competitions, power in a jumper, movement for a dressage horse – and a Thoroughbred which has the ideal build for racing, for example, was never intended to make a top-class dressage horse because it doesn't have the power in its back and quarters for collected work (though there will always be exceptions to the rule: a case in point being the ex-racehorse Wily Trout, which competed in dressage with Chris Bartle at international level).

Obviously, the breed of a horse will determine to a certain extent its size and temperament, and riders should consider how well their own height and build suits the horse. The German horses are really well made and quite strong and so may not be suitable for a lady rider (though there are probably some lady riders who are stronger than some men!). I find they need much more work on the flat and can produce something of a battle because of their strength. Belgian-bred horses are also quite strong rides. Emma-Jane Mac copes very well with her Belgian-bred, Everest Gringo, and is particularly good against the clock, even though he takes a strong hold. The Irish horses are finer and make good jumping horses as they are easier to ride than some of the German horses. Both Clover and Silver Dust are Irish-bred; Silver Dust is a slightly more thick-set horse with real jumping power. Clover, being finer in build, excels in speed classes because of his agility. Some of the Thoroughbred x Irish Draught horses are ideal for showjumping: Thoroughbred blood gives them agility and athleticism to cope with combination fences, and speed which is essential for competitions against the clock; and the Irish Draught gives enormous strength in the back and quarters for pure jumping power, also physical and mental toughness, and a generous, kind temperament – the Irish Draught commutes the Thoroughbred's tendency to excitability.

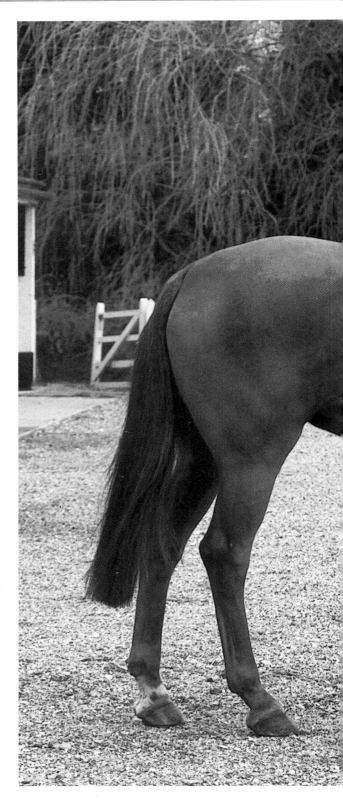

selecting

This stallion has all the right credentials for a show-jumper. His shoulders and hindquarters show power and strength at both ends

selecting

Dutch horses are usually quite rideable and are similar to the Irish in breeding. Joe Turi's stallion, Vital, is Dutch-bred and this combination has won many classes including the Hickstead Derby in 1990. Annette Miller's Tutein and her Zephyrus are also Dutch-bred. French horses are more Thoroughbred in build and temperament, and I find are probably the most excitable of all – they have a certain way of going, and they don't suit the majority of riders: I always say you need a Frenchman to ride a French horse! Having said that, they are very agile and do not lack speed in the arena; and they jump so economically that it is a wonder they don't have more fences down – though that, of course, is where they make up against the clock. Pierre Durand's Jappeloup, although only 15.2hh, was a great example of 'flair française'. This outstanding little horse cer-tainly captured the spectators' hearts, rather like Milton, because of his athleticism. Jappeloup was out of a Thoroughbred mare, by a trotter called Tyrol II; he was definitely quite a character and certainly far from easy to ride.

The upshot of these various observations is that although I do not go for one particular breed when I am looking to buy a horse, I do find it is worth considering some breeds rather than others because typically these possess certain qualities of physique or temperament that I would prefer in my showjumper. Generally therefore, I am looking for a 'nice cut of a horse' with an honest character – and this question of temperament is crucial, as there is nothing worse than being in constant battle with a horse, particularly if the rider is inexperienced, because nine times out of ten it is the horse which emerges the winner.

 # Temperament

It seems to me that many prospective horse buyers place an inordinate emphasis on conformation when it comes to buying showjumpers. Certainly there should be no obvious defects in the horse's physical structure which might cause long-term problems, but the first priority for the showjumping rider is that the horse clears the jumps. There are no points for pretty faces but there *is* prize money for jumping consistent clear rounds! Just like a car, the bodywork may be very pleasing to look at, but if the engine does not run smoothly and pull well, then it is as good as useless.

Thus, in my own experience, I have found that one of the first considerations should be the horse's temperament and attitude. A horse that is willing to please and is prepared to try hard for its rider is much more likely to do well as compared to one that might have lovely paces but shows little or no desire to co-operate with its rider. Moreover, a showjumping horse should enjoy what it is doing: there is no better example of this than Milton, who is a trier through and through because he just loves to jump – he wants to jump, he wants to please and this is why he is a top-class horse. Person-ally I prefer geldings to mares because I find their attitude more reliable; and I like Irish or Thoroughbred horses. Silver Dust is Irish and we seem to 'click' well together.

So if a horse is going to succeed, it must be a trier and have the initiative to think for itself at times. There are many horses that simply jump because they have been told to, but do not really fire on all cylinders: these horses will always lack that bit of sparkle and will never pull out that extra little bit which will get them into the higher category. There are umpteen Grade B horses in Britain, proving that many are quite capable of reaching a certain standard in the BSJA grading system – but only a handful of these have that extra something which will make them good Grade A showjumpers: they are the talented few, and it's as simple as that!

Having said that, if a horse has the right temperament and it looks good *as well*, the ingredients for success are immediately doubled – the more 'correct' his physical shape, the more easily he will cope with the work we require of him, and our chances of making the most of any jumping ability must therefore be improved.

Conformation

When I go to view a horse, I like to take a good look at its physical make-up – its conformation – without the saddle first. The first thing I would look for in a potential show-jumping horse is a good honest head which shows some intelligence, not carried too high, with a kind eye that denotes a gentle and willing temperament. A shoulder with a slope of about 45° helps to create more flowing activity in the front legs, and means the horse will be able to shorten and lengthen its stride with relative ease; any more upright and the leg action will tend to be choppy, and will jarr into the ground – not something we want when landing over big fences!

The neck should be fairly long, tapering into the head: if the neck is upside-down, and too thick at the gullet, the horse will find it harder to 'make a shape' over a jump, and to keep its balance. Watch a horse jump: it will lower its head and stretch its neck out to judge its take-off; in flight its head should be lowered so that it can arch its back and thus more tidily clear the fence; and it brings its head up on landing as its hocks push further under its bodyweight to re-balance it on the flat. A 'coupled' back which is not too short and not too long is ideal for jumping. Horses with long backs are far more difficult to supple, and therefore it isn't easy to achieve a great degree of collection with them. Without engagement from the back legs, the horse can very easily become 'hollow' in the back, and this will cause the head to be raised and the stride to shorten – the horse will end up running around with its nose in the air.

Silver Dust is an excellent example of near-perfect conformation for a showjumper: a real power horse with strength all round. He has a kind, honest face, sturdy legs and really powerful hindquarters. Dusty is definitely one to excel in the 'big' classes

Like Silver Dust, Clover is Irish bred, but is much finer in build. Clover is a great horse against the clock so I enter him in speed competitions. He is slightly larger in the leg than Silver Dust and covers the ground well
Inset: I like to see kind eyes and an alert expression in any horse. A good horse will be co-operative and should enjoy jumping

Ideally the horse must have strong loins, and its hindquarters should be rounded and powerful, with good large hip joints and hocks. It is important that it has no leg problems – a horse with thickened or contracted tendons should be discarded immediately! I like to see a horse that is long in the forearm but short in the cannon: this sort of leg will stand up to jumping on a regular basis. A horse with longer legs is more susceptible to strains and knocks than one with short, strong cannon bones and tendons which are extremely effective shock absorbers when jumping.

Good foot structure is vital: when landing over a fence the foot, and particularly the frog, takes much of the concussion. Look for nice flat heels with a good frog and bars – the foot when lifted up, should be saucer-shaped and concave; and beware of flat soles.

Silver Dust is an excellent stamp of a horse when it comes to the ideal conformation for a showjumper: he has a real powerful look about him and can be wound up like a spring, giving him a better chance of clearing a big parallel, or coming through a big combination without touching a pole.

There is invariably a great deal of generalising when discussing conformation: but as always, it comes down to the fact that if the horse has the right attitude and is keen to jump, it is this enthusiasm which counts, whatever its shape and size. The best example of this has got to be Towerlands Anglezarke who has (and I am sure Malcolm Pyrah won't mind me saying this!) the worst pair of hocks on a horse that probably anyone has ever seen; he shuffles along and dishes in front – but no-one could ever dispute his brilliance in the showjumping arena. John Whitaker's Ryan's Son was a very plain horse, as was my father's Olympic Star. You probably wouldn't give them a second look turned out at grass, but they possessed real talent in the arena. I think it is a bonus to have a horse with classic conformation and good looks that can also win major showjumping competitions, which is why Milton is really quite outstanding; he has all these attributes, and the crowd loves him.

If the horse is unbroken it is more difficult to judge how it will perform, and there is a world of difference as far as maturity is concerned between, for example, a two- and a three-year-old. This is where conformation is important, and an experienced eye can usually judge how a two-year-old will mature. When I am looking at unbroken horses I can, as a norm, quickly rule out the ones that I don't like – maybe they have an obviously mean or timid temperament, or they move in a way which will be difficult to train – too clumsy, they knock themselves, or they are too extravagant. However, there are always a few that go on and prove me wrong! If possible, have a horse led out in hand and trotted up on a hard surface; this gives some indication of how it moves and I like to watch it from all angles. It can also be useful to watch a horse being loose-schooled or lunged over jumps; however, although many young horses will jump on the lunge quite nicely without a rider, often their style will change when under saddle.

Movement

It is always very pleasing to see a horse that moves well, but in the case of a young jumping horse, it can actually be detrimental to its jumping style if it moves too straight. Normally, it is best to choose a horse that has free, elastic paces as opposed to very straight and 'showy' ones which sometimes incline the horse to be rather less quick in snapping up his legs over a fence. An athletic type of horse is required for jumping, that doesn't 'dish' too much in front, and one that is level in its paces. I like to see free movement in the shoulder so that the horse can use its scope to maximum effect, yet can still tuck its legs under well as it goes over a jump. A young horse will probably not be all that supple, but with time and exercise, its muscles will build up and its athleticism increase.

The horse is working well in the draw reins without becoming overbent. We have a flowing 'active' trot, and the horse is concentrating on the job in hand and listening to my aids

It is always a good idea for the prospective buyer to watch a horse being ridden before he tries it out himself, paying careful attention to its way of going and its temperament. Does it show courage and independence, going forward willingly? Or is it nappy and obstinate? Is it naughty – does it buck? Many people maintain that a horse which bucks well will jump well, because this indicates a strong back. Will it be too excitable for a show situation – perhaps it hots up after a canter? Is it spooky? Again, some consider that a horse which spooks will make a careful jumper. If it rushes off, is this because it is excitable, or because it has obviously been frightened at some point? If it stops, is this because it is young and inexperienced, or because it is mean and nappy – in which case you won't want it. Is it quick and athletic? Or gauche and clumsy – and if so, will this improve as the horse matures, or is it the result of poor conformation?

After you have watched it being ridden for a while, then you might get on its back and try it out. Remember that if the horse is a youngster, it may not have had any real experience of jumping at this stage, and its muscles will not be fully developed. All these factors need to be taken into consideration when assessing a horse's potential. Some people do loose-school their horses when they are young but I would not entirely judge a horse's jumping ability by watching it without a rider. I would rather see a horse, being ridden, jumping a foot high than see one jumping six feet high loose. It is amazing what a difference a rider makes – and not always for the better!

As a horse matures, so its style and action may change through both muscle and mental development. Nevertheless, if a horse jumps with a natural bascule, so much the better, as Mother Nature did not particularly design him with jumping in mind: a horse has 18 pairs of ribs, which means he doesn't have sufficient space between his rib cage and pelvis to be a natural jumper (unlike dogs, which have only 13, and cats 11 pairs). This means that to showjump successfully, a horse must be taught to jump in a certain way – he must 'bascule', that is, he must use his head and neck to round his back, enabling him to tuck up his legs and feet more easily. If he jumps naturally in this way, he will obviously be easier to train, and will himself find the work easier to cope with. And again, some horses love the idea of jumping and others despise it, so an important part of the selection process is assessing the horse's courage and enthusiasm. Stroller, Marion Coake's famous international showjumper, stood only 14.2hh but he had a natural bascule when jumping, and he had tremendous courage: it is because he had both of these qualities that he was so outstanding. This is also true of Milton; he has a brilliant natural style so he finds showjumping easy, and he loves to show off – his enthusiasm for the job is written all over his face.

Some jumping problems can be corrected with proper training, but personally I would always prefer to know that the basic qualities and temperament I have mentioned were there. For example, a horse that rushes its fences, or becomes excitable when jumping, can often be calmed by means of 'placing poles' and various schooling exercises (we will discuss these later); but horses that are nervy and easily frightened should be avoided however good they look – they very rarely listen to reason, and are likely to find the atmosphere at shows mind-blowing. Likewise, nappy horses will not usually change their ways for any length of time, and are quite likely to get fed-up with jumping and turn bolshy. Having said all this, there is nothing wrong with a horse that has character – take Ryan's Son, for example, whose characteristic bucks became part of his arena performance; but this did not mean that he was particularly awkward or lacked scope – he was an outstanding horse. Further, both Jappeloup and Milton (two of the most talented horses of all time) are playful and excitable, but they love jumping – and that is what matters.

Sometimes the prospective horse buyer will hear of good horses for sale by word of mouth; otherwise he can look through equestrian magazines, all of which carry an enormous number of advertisements for horses and ponies for sale. These should be read with a certain degree of caution however, because some of the descriptions are inaccurate and disillusioning, to say the least. There is nothing more exasperating than travelling miles in response to an advertisement, to find that the animal which is led out is nothing like its description. Generally, it is best to approach a *reputable* horse dealer: at this sort of establishment there is more likely to be a variety of horses to choose from, and it will be in the dealer's interest to try and find the rider a horse that he or she thinks will be suitable. Young horses vary enormously in price, depending on their breeding and the demand for a particular type of horse. Some people are lucky and can pick up a youngster that proves to be a natural for as little as £1,500. It is impossible to generalise where prices are concerned but a proven Grade A could fetch hundreds of thousands of pounds – it is amazing how much people will pay in pursuit of success. More realistically, your average young 'hopeful' may be anything from £4–10,000 – probably more for one with good breeding. It is a false economy to try and save money by buying the cheapest horse if it is not what the rider really wants; and equally, even the most expensive young horse may never suit a certain type of rider – once again, how important it is that there isn't a personality clash between horse and rider!

It isn't a good idea to buy the first horse you see; have a look at a few and think it over properly. The most important thing is to like the horse you are considering, in particular its character and outlook on life, and to feel a definite empathy with it: if you cannot establish a mutual understanding it is unlikely to perform well for you. I always like to think that I develop a bond with my horses, and in this way get the best results. And remember that a horse which goes well for one rider may not necessarily be suitable for another; too many people rush into buying a horse because they have seen it jumping well for somebody else. However, to assume that it will continue to do so for a different rider is a mistake, and to buy on performance record alone is probably a false security.

Obviously if the horse has a bloodline with good showjumping credentials, the chances are that it, too, will have a talent for jumping, as long as the rider has sufficient knowledge to train it. Grandeur and the younger Quito de Baussy, Moet et Chandon Prince and Quiddam are all stallions of proven ability used with the express purpose of breeding jumpers. In fact, Franke Sloothaak's grey mare Gina Ginelli is one to watch for the future – her sire is Thomas Fruhmann's Grandeur. Many young horses are ruined because they have been handled by inexperienced riders who think they can manage without assistance. This is a great shame, because once a horse develops a phobia about jumping, it is difficult to overcome the problem. On the other hand, for the more experienced, buying unbroken youngstock has its advantages because by and large these are less likely to have been ruined through mishandling.

Finally, I never buy a horse without getting it vetted, first and foremost because it really is never worth the risk. If a horse is going to compete well it needs to be sound in every way, and the vet is by far the best judge of this.

The vet will check the horse for soundness in heart, wind, limb and eye and will also include the identity of the horse, its age, height and any signs of disease or injury. He is giving a guarantee that the horse is sound on that particular day, however, and is not judging the horse's character and temperament, but he can give his opinion as to whether the horse is 'fit' for the job in question. It is wise to take your own vet who will give you his honest opinion on the horse. If you are paying a substantial amount of money, it may be worth having the horse's legs X-rayed and its blood tested; always be wary of owners who refuse to let this happen, as they may have something to hide.

The key to success in any yard – whether it is dressage, eventing or showjumping – is undoubtedly good stable management. Good general stable management really is the foundation of a horse's well-being, and if he feels great he will try harder in the arena; so we try to help all our horses as much as possible in this respect by working out a training and feeding programme to suit each individual. Horses are essentially creatures of habit and seem to have an infallibly accurate sense of time that tells them exactly when they should expect to be fed and ridden, turned out or brought in. A disruption of routine can quite unsettle some horses, and this is the last thing anybody wants when they are competing. However, we find that it works best for us to follow a fairly rigid routine, and we stick to it as closely as possible. If I am competing this can sometimes get quite difficult, as classes are always held at different times of the day – some first thing in the morning, others late in the evening – but although we have to adapt our normal routine, we still try to keep to it if we can at shows. The success with which this is accomplished, is entirely due to the dedication and hard work of my groom, Gill Baines, who has devoted herself to my horses and has run the yard at Quendon with incomparable efficiency for a long time. At home Gill feeds our horses at the same time each day, and during competitions she still tries to keep our feeding routine as close in time and similar in content to their normal day-to-day regime as she can.

Such a conscientious approach is not only relevant to feeding and training: if we are not very careful to look after every detail in our stable management, whether it concerns basic hygiene, maintenance of tack and equipment, or the horse's health, our neglect could well compromise the success of our showjumper, be it a potential or proven competition animal. Bad and untidy stable management also reflects on the yard: at Quendon we therefore always do our best to keep everything as tidy as possible.

The perennial rule is that every horse is different according to temperament, breeding and maturity, and so work programmes and feeding requirements should always be worked out according to these characteristics. So how does your horse feel when he is really fit and well? Probably tremendously strong and bouncy when you are riding him; his coat sleek and shining, his eye bright; the muscles in his quarters and neck well-defined and hard, and not too much tummy; when hacking out he may pull a bit, or give a squeal and a buck. Knowing all this, and understanding your horse, is of paramount importance because if a rider knows his horse well, he will

There is no better way of letting horses relax than turning them out in the field for a couple of hours a day to kick up their heels

selecting

know exactly how it feels when it is fit and healthy and will recognise when it is slightly off-colour; then problems of, say, viral illness or lameness which are just in their beginnings can be nipped in the bud and with any luck prevented.

There is no better way of building up the young horse's confidence than through his daily handling in the stable. His early experiences are crucial, and when grooming him, picking out his feet, tacking him up – in all the day-to-day routine jobs – we must show him that he can trust his rider: he needs to be absolutely sure that we are not going to do anything that will frighten or harm him. This does not mean he can get away with bad habits in the stable; pushy, over-confident youngsters that are allowed to barge into you, bite and chew, and be generally unmannerly, will invariably turn out nappy and obstinate when ridden. But if he has been handled quietly and sensibly as a youngster, this must be a good step along the way to a happy and successful partnership.

At Quendon we have established a daily routine which is as follows:

7am	Water, feed and muck out and sweep up the yard.
8.45am	The horses are put on the horse-walker to loosen up for about twenty minutes.
9.05am	Horses are ridden, each one schooled for half an hour, followed by half an hour's hack. Each horse is groomed after being ridden, and turned out in the field for a couple of hours to relax.
1pm	Mid-day feed; clean tack; groom horses again; skip the stables out; cleaning and other odd jobs.
4.30pm	Muck out and check water.
5pm	Main feed (with added vitamins); sweep up the yard; check the feed-bins are full.
9pm	Check the horses are warm and comfortable for the night; check the water and haynets.

There are no hard and fast rules as far as feeding is concerned – what is good for one horse may not necessarily work for another and too much feed can have catastrophic effects both in terms of behaviour and physical fitness – namely azoturia. Besides, a showjumper probably won't require such high levels of feeding as, for example, an event horse, because his jumping courses are shorter and so great stamina is not a pre-requisite; nor will he have to gallop at great speed. Therefore the work the horse does and the food he eats are completely interdependent; and the sort of food he is given depends on a number of other factors, too – his type (breeding), his character, his age, the time of year, even the weather. For example, spring grass is full of protein and will make horses feel 'full of beans', so hard feed may well have to be reduced to prevent the horse – and particularly a youngster – becoming naughty. In cold weather he will probably be far more 'on his toes'; when it is hot, horribly lazy. If the horse tends to be overweight he won't need fattening feed such as barley, unlike a thin type who will – some horses can eat hay, barley, sugarbeet, all the weight-producing foods ad lib and still not look big and well! We tend to feed Clover more fattening foods because he has a tendency to lose weight quickly; he is more of a 'worrier' than Vanessa and Silver Dust. Silver Dust doesn't get any barley because he is naturally well-built and puts weight on very easily, which can make him quite lazy. When we have young horses we try not to feed them anything too 'heating' such as oats, as they tend to be quite 'keyed up' to start with anyway; and a Thoroughbred horse is going to be more excitable than an Irish Draught and so they must be fed accordingly.

As a general rule, the diet of our stabled horses in competition would basically consist of bran, nuts, chop and sugarbeet, fed three times a day. This provides a balanced diet, the bran and hay supplying a very good source of roughage to clear their systems, the nuts and sugarbeet protein and carbohydrate for energy. A horse in moderate work will receive approximately 50 per cent concentrates with 50 per cent hay; our competition horses can receive up to 70 per cent concentrates and 30 per cent hay. In the main evening feed Gill always gives extra vitamins, in particular vitamin E and selenium and salt which assists the digestion of protein. If any of the horses have been competing or working particularly hard, we will offer them electrolytes in case they have become dehydrated. The electrolytes also help to replace the minerals lost when a horse sweats a lot, for example during competition – this is particularly useful for young horses who may well sweat quite freely with excitement and anticipation when they first go to competitions. Feed supplements are really a matter of personal choice; there are so many feed supplements available that it can be very difficult to decide which are the most effective.

Inevitably there will be some trial and error in feeding any horse, but it is most important ultimately to arrive at the right balance of feed for the individual horse, and to learn how and when to adapt it to *keep* it right for *him*. If a horse is fed too much of the wrong sort of food for his particular type and temperament, it can actually do him more harm than good.

The work-related ration

As our young horses get fitter, we can increase their feed in line with the increased amount of exercise they are receiving, though even horses working at the same level will vary in the amount of work they need to achieve the desired standard, and this will also dictate what feed they will need. For example an older horse – over 12 years – takes longer to get fit than an 8 or 9 year-old and will probably need more food to keep him sharp. A keen, Thoroughbred-type horse is easy to get fit but may be inclined to run up rather light, and will therefore need a lot of hay, and nuts and barley but not oats; whereas a lazy horse – the part-bred type you have to 'chase' the whole time to make him do a decent bit of work – should not be given too much hay, or stodgy food such as barley or coarse mix, but could be revved up with a few oats!

Some horses, particularly older ones, need competitions to keep them sharp – whatever you feed them, they get bored with the day-to-day schooling and need an outing to make them exert themselves. Some perform better the fresher they are, and really only need to go 'out' once; some need two or three outings. So you must know your horse if your preparations are aimed at one important occasion.

Reducing the feed

Once the horse is really fit and his muscle built up he is less likely to need long periods of training to keep him at his peak. If you continue with a full workload you risk pushing him 'over the top' and he will just turn sour. A competition horse is almost bound to get stale at some point – most horses will only take so much training whether they are novices or Grade As, though the more experienced ones tend to reach this point more quickly than the youngster for whom everything is 'new'. This is when a horse is most likely to go off his feed, and if he does it is vital to *reduce* his hard feed and even let him miss out entirely for a couple of days. Hay and a bit of grass are quite sufficient to keep him performing at the same level for a short time once he *is* fit. Make sure the manger is spotlessly clean, and when you re-introduce hard feed, start with tiny quantities and build up gradually. Every horse has its own limit anyway, and most fit horses become more 'picky' if you try and push them to eat more than they want.

Hay

All feed should be of the best quality, and this is particularly important with hay which if dusty or mouldy can cause serious respiratory problems. Some people see nothing wrong in buying cheaper foods for their horses; however, if these lack goodness and quality, their horses are never going to reach peak fitness and condition. If the hay is in the least dusty the horse will cough: in this case the hay ration can be soaked in water for 12hrs in a plastic dustbin, otherwise silage-type forage can be used. This is completely dust-free but is much higher in protein than hay so the hard feed should be correspondingly reduced.

How much hay to give depends on each horse – the light types that tend to run up can usually have as much as they want, given three times a day so that the ration is always fresh; those that put on a hundredweight on even a small ration are severely restricted. A horse working towards a big competition must have a tighter stomach so his ration would be reduced overnight as the big day approaches.

Buy enough hay to last the summer and autumn seasons: it is not a good idea to change hay in the middle of the horse's competition year – the change to a different variety or mixture could induce colic or coughing – and new hay should not be fed until at least October of the same year; and if you are not quick, farmers will have brought their new hay in and buried the old at the back of the stack.

Keep it clean!

Not only must the horse's food be free from dirt and dust, but the buckets or mangers from which he eats and drinks must also be kept spotlessly clean. Wipe each manger round thoroughly with a wisp of clean hay after use, to minimise the risk of infection from mouldy foodstuffs — besides, how would you like eating your meal off a dirty plate? Nothing is more likely to put a finicky feeder off his food.

Water

I like to see horses drink a good deal of water: 8 to 12gal (36–54l) should be the average daily consumption for a horse; this flushes out his system and prevents him from becoming dehydrated; by letting him drink when he feels like it, he will usually maintain the correct fluid intake. We provide each horse with a salt lick, which encourages them to drink more and supplies important minerals to their blood. All our stables are equipped with automatic water feeders, which seem to work well, though some people prefer to use buckets so they can monitor exactly how much water their horses are drinking. Again, the water must be fresh and clean, and so must the water container.

Setbacks to fitness

A good rider and horseman will know his horse and be conscious of how he should feel all the time he is training him; in this way he will notice straightaway if something is wrong, and with luck, problems can be nipped in the bud. Maybe the horse feels less bouncy than usual, pulls less, or blows or sweats more than he should and this could indicate that he is incubating a viral infection. Stop work and reduce his feed straightaway; to continue working him will strain, even damage heart and lungs.

The most dreaded injury is a damaged tendon or ligament; even a minor strain means the horse must be rested for 6 weeks. Check his legs night and morning: if there is the *least* sign of heat or swelling that isn't usually there, and isn't an obvious knock or bump, stop work and cut down feed immediately. The worst thing you can do is to carry on as normal in the hope that these particular symptoms might disappear, because you will almost certainly make a slight strain – a matter of rest for a few weeks – into a serious one, where the tendon might be so damaged that your showjumper's career is finished for ever.

You can just wait and see how quickly it goes down, or you can call the vet who may suggest that you have the injury scanned.

If the leg goes down within a day or two, you could resume *light* work; if it does not, or if there is any bow in the tendon, the horse must be laid off for at least 6 months.

The treatments are various, but are all without heat. Therefore you can use a hose, ice packs, Wurly boots, proprietary cooling lotion, cold Animalintex, alternate ice and pressure bandages. If the horse is very lame it must be box-rested; but lead it out in hand if at all possible to keep the blood circulating.

The showjumper's joints are subjected to greater stress than horses competing in other disciplines, and are particularly susceptible when the horse is asked to jump and turn at speed in a restricted area such as the

showjumping ring. If the young horse is entered for speed classes too early in his career or too soon for his level of training, before his physical frame is really mature and sufficiently hardened up, he is quite likely to incur injury. This is often in the hock and can appear as bursal swelling, thoroughpin or curb, all indicating strain. With rest these injuries may sort themselves out and cold laser treatment can be most effective; but as with any strain, if you continue, the damage could become established and serious.

As much as possible should always be done to ease jarring to the horse's legs and joints, particularly as the ground is so often hard for the showjumping season. We try to avoid jumping on hard ground, particularly with the young horses. Gill uses a cooling gel on their legs prior to a competiton, and an Ice-Tight paste after jumping. Your farrier could fit concussion pads under the horse's shoes and you should always be very fussy about the going both at home and in the show ring. Where possible you should insist on watering or the provision of sand, or rotovating where necessary.

Muscle damage is quite a common problem, though a proper training programme with a gradual build up of work should help prevent muscle injuries. However, in the event of such injury, various measures can be employed: cold laser and ultrasonic machines (eg magneta pulse blanket); a Faradic machine (a pad that emits an electronic impulse; this treatment brings a damaged muscle out of spasm, and can bring remarkably quick improvement); and most important of all, rest.

A common problem in jumping horses – and particularly showjumpers – and one which is not always recognised as such, is the formation of a knot of muscle in the lumbar column just behind the withers. This is caused by concussion, and can be provoked even when the going is good; it arises simply as a result of the horse landing time and

selecting

again over fences – essentially an unnatural practice for any horse.

You may notice that the horse is moving with a shorter stride than usual, particularly downhill; he may start to 'pop in a short one' before a fence rather than standing off, even a little; he may even start refusing. A horse physiotherapist will normally be able to sort out the problem, either by manipulation and massage, or with a Faradic machine.

Azoturia is a stiffening/cramp of the muscles in the loins and hindquarters and is more common than many of us would care to admit. It is usually caused when the horse is fed too much – particularly heating food such as oats and barley – for the amount of work

he is doing. Thus azoturia is most likely after a day off; after a long journey; or after an injury entailing enforced rest.

Basically prevention is better than cure, and if for any reason the horse must rest, cut his feed ration in half and feed plenty of bran. Some horses do seem more prone to azoturia than others. It can also be selenium deficiency in which case feed a vitamin supplement containing selenium; a tbsp of bicarbonate of soda in the evening feed also helps.

Jumping inflicts an enormous amount of concussion on the horse's joints, and so we are very careful about the conditions under which we jump our horses

Stables and bedding

We stable most of our horses in loose boxes and they have a good view of everything that is going on around them. I like them to be able to look out over their stable doors so they can get as much fresh air as possible; Quendon is a busy yard, and having plenty to look at also prevents them from becoming too bored and developing stable vices such as crib-biting, windsucking or weaving. Going out in the field every day for a while also helps to prevent boredom and its related vices.

Gone are the days when there was just straw to bed down horses; we can now buy a variety of bedding materials including shavings, peat, sawdust and even shredded paper. Whichever bedding is used it must be mucked out at regular intervals throughout the day so that the horse has a dry bed free from droppings; this will encourage him to lie down and rest, and prevent problems in the feet (namely thrush). We always use shavings for our horses because they are less likely to cause respiratory problems because of inhaled or ingested dust. Any horse which coughs because it is vulnerable to inhaled dust should not really be bedded with straw because straw produces a much great infestation of dust spores which persist in the atmosphere; and if the horse coughs or for some reason is thick in the wind, it must be false economy to buy bedding which will hinder its performance, however cheap it maybe. Deep litter shavings provide a good soft bed and are easy to keep clean; we always make sure the sides of the stables are banked up well to try and prevent the horses getting themselves cast if they roll.

Grooming

We find that grooming is best done 'little and often'. In the morning before they are ridden our horses are quartered – a quick 'once over' with a body brush to make sure there are not bits of dirt or bedding in the coat which might lodge under the tack and rub – and again after their exercise; they are then turned out in the field for a couple of hours to relax and enjoy themselves. If it is cold or very muddy they will wear a New Zealand rug and a hood; these do save hours of work! Gill will then give them a thorough grooming in the evening, before they are rugged up again. She has her work cut out with Silver Dust who prefers to look like 'Gold Dust' after he has been rolling! We will use a summer sheet during the warm weather, and a light breathable rug when the horses are travelling. Our sponsor's day rugs are used for special occasions. Not only does grooming make the horses look presentable and provide a good way of initially handling the youngsters, it also tones up the muscles, and is an important part of their 'body-building' programme. Strapping a horse really does benefit the muscles – in America, race-horses are strapped by immensely powerful men with a weight-lifter's physique, specifically employed for this very job; it also brings a really good, deep shine to the coat. Manes and tails are pulled regularly to keep them looking tidy and respectable, and we may start clipping towards the end of August, beginning of September as the horses' winter coats start to grow through.

Pulling and plaiting

We don't always plait a horse's mane and tail for a show; though when we do we plait with needle and thread because it looks neater and will stay in longer. Otherwise, however, I do like manes and tails to look tidy and clean and by pulling them regularly, taking just a few hairs at a time from the underside, it is easy to keep everything looking neat. Some young horses object strongly to having mane and tail pulled; obviously, the skin is very sensitive, so never take big chunks to hurry the job along because this will be extremely painful. The best time to pull a mane or tail is after the horse has been worked and is still quite warm; the pores will be open and the hair can be pulled out much more easily, making the whole process less distressing to the horse. Damp the mane and tail down every day to encourage the hair to lie flat;

hair gel also works well for this job. It is common sense that when pulling a tail you don't stand where the horse can kick you – some people manage to pull their horse's tail over the top of a stable door but this is not always possible if the horse is small or fidgety and the door high.

Always be conscious of the fact that the appearance and turnout of horse and rider are a reflection on the yard from whence they came: clean, tidy and shining – fit, healthy and enthusiastic – such a pleasing impression can only indicate that every conceivable effort is being devoted to the care of the horse.

Vaccination

It is absolutely essential that a competition horse's equine influenza passport is correctly filled in, with accurate diagram and written description, and that the injections have been given with the correct interval of days between the first *three of the primary* course, and then the boosters kept up to date at yearly intervals (364 days). Any mistake, any one injection late by one day – even in the primary course – and the horse will be denied access to *any* affiliated competition and nowadays most show-grounds; the innocu-

lation course will then have to be started again. We work it so that the annual boosters for tetanus (every two years) and 'flu are given during the Christmas period when the horses are not so busy.

I also like the horses' teeth to be checked every year and rasped when necessary so as to avoid unnecessary digestive or mouth problems; and they have a regular worming programme – this is generally every 6 weeks, ringing the changes with the type of wormer used to prevent worm resistance.

Shoeing

The old adage 'no foot, no horse' is never so true than when it concerns jumpers, since the foot must absorb the force of the horse's whole bodyweight as it lands after a fence. Correct balance of the foot is vital: if the toe is too long there will be more strain put on the tendons; if the horse is shod too tight this will eventually cause contracted heels, and the heels and frog will not then be fully effective in absorbing the shock of landing, resulting in undue stress 'passed back' to the leg.

Corrective Shoeing

A horse that brushes or speedy cuts may well end up performing below his best unless his action can be corrected: often he will knock himself on a turn, resulting in a momentary loss of impulsion and balance and therefore not such a good jump over the next fence: maybe a rolled pole for 4 faults. In this case a farrier can fit $^3/4$ shoes; or he can bevel the inside edge of the shoe, or take back the toe.

Studs

Nowadays it must be almost unknown for a horse to jump and not wear studs to do so: small sharp ones for hard ground, larger squarer ones when the going is muddy or at all deep. Some horses wear two on each foot; those that tuck up their forearm very tight as they jump will need to wear a leather 'apron' – a piece of leather which attaches to the girth and prevents the studs cutting the horse's belly. The farrier will fit the stud holes and thread them. He can also re-shoe a horse just before a show with large-headed nails, in the same way that a racehorse is plated; this is good for hard conditions when studs could make the balance of the foot uneven and thus cause unnecessary strain to the landing leg.

 # Pasture and maintenance

All our horses are turned out and allowed to graze for a couple of hours each day, so we are careful to ensure that the grass is of good quality and the pasture well-maintained. A mixture based on perennial ryegrass and white clover, together with timothy and some of the coarser meadow fescues is best. It is always a good practice to graze horses with sheep, at a ratio of 10 sheep to one horse; sheep will keep the grass short and evenly grazed so the horses are less likely to dung all in corner, and they help to keep the field clear

of worm eggs. Weeds and thistles will need topping over; poisonous plants, and particularly ragwort should be pulled up from the roots and destroyed by burning; otherwise remove it from the field because dead ragwort is even more poisonous to the horse than when it is alive — and cutting it is pointless because it will very quickly grow through again.

Droppings should be removed from the field regularly – at least twice a week – to prevent the grass becoming sour; this good practice also reduces the pasture's inevitable worm-burden, so easily transmitted to horses – particularly if sheep cannot be kept.

The field should be checked regularly for potentially injurious sharp objects lying about such as broken glass, tin cans or old bits of car or bicycle which might have been thrown over the fence, particularly if a road runs alongside. Some people seem to think that 'Keep Britain Tidy' means throwing their litter over the nearest hedge!

Fences should be carefully maintained. Post and rail fencing is the best for horses; though wire fencing is seen everywhere – rusty, slack, with spare coils all over the place it is potentially lethal and even taut, well-maintained wire fences have frequently been known to cause frightful injury. Horses, and particularly youngsters, are not clever at all where fencing is concerned and seem to get caught and tangled up at the least excuse; so take every possible care and precaution.

All our paddocks are fenced with posts and rails, and by sectioning off fields we are able to rotate the grazing to allow the pasture to 'rest'. All too often we see horses in fields with inadequate fencing – they are literally grazing in a danger zone. A well fenced and properly maintained field is a small price to pay in comparison to injuring a horse for life

Tack and equipment

For any sort of training, the saddlery and protective equipment should be chosen and put on correctly. Tack should be maintained in good condition — riding a young horse can have its nerve-wracking moments, and doesn't need the added hazard of tack breaking! Serious accidents have happened through reins and stirrup leathers snapping, and tack should be inspected regularly. Today there is an enormous range of products to choose from, particularly for protecting the horse's back and legs; these vary in price and quality, but I would always advise investing in good quality tack and equipment. This doesn't mean you have to pay the earth, but it is never worth buying something of inferior quality.

There will always be a certain amount of trial and error in selecting the sort of tack required for a young horse. Time will tell how the horse will behave, and you must work out the necessary tack and equipment to have sufficient control. You will need to assess what tack your horse will perform in best, especially where bits and nosebands are concerned. It is sensible to borrow equipment and find out if it actually works, before rushing out to your nearest saddler and spending a lot of money unnecessarily. A well schooled horse should not need too many gadgets; although I do not believe in constantly struggling with a horse, the better disciplined it is, the simpler your tack should be.

 # Boots

🐎 Tendon boots are essential to protect the horse's legs. The boots shown here have a good lining so that they do not rub or cause soreness, and they cover the tendons adequately. It is worth investing in a good pair that fit properly. Always make sure the fastenings are secure and are not likely to come undone while you are schooling

A young horse should wear tendon or brushing boots which will protect his front legs, and over-reach boots to prevent damage to heels. If the horse is being lunged, he will need tendon boots behind as well because he is more likely to speedy-cut (strike into himself above the fetlock). If he is being

ridden, then tendon boots on the front with fetlock boots on the hind legs should provide adequate protection. Over-reach boots are particularly useful in the early stages because the horse will still be accustoming himself to the weight of the rider and finding his balance when schooling; he will be on his forehand and more likely to knock himself.

Boots and elastic support bandages must be put on carefully because if they are put on too tightly or so as to cause uneven pressure on the leg they will rub and may even result in swelling and strain. I prefer the tendon boots with the sheepskin lining because they are less likely to rub if the boots are worn for any length of time.

Open-fronted tendon boots are often used for the showjumper; if he knocks a pole in front the rap on his cannon may persuade him to be more careful next time.

🐎 The young horse is fitted with a flash noseband and gentle bit. The noseband provides the back-up 'control system' to the bit, and this particular type is ideal for jumping because it is a useful aid to the rider in the arena where good 'steering' is required!

s e l e c t i n g

38

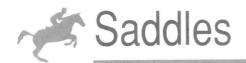

Saddles

For preference, the saddle should have a forward-cut style so the rider is not too 'deep' and can adopt the more forward 'jumping' position with relative ease; it should be made from a good quality leather. There are now a number of 'close contact' saddles on the market, and many of our showjumping riders use these; they really do give the rider a better contact with the horse. I would always recommend that an experienced saddler comes out to fit the saddle to the individual horse. If it is looked after properly, a saddle will last a long time so it is worth spending a little extra to get it right, and the rider will need to be comfortable as well as the horse so the saddle must fit both.

Saddle cloths or numnahs should be used under the saddle to protect the horse's back. A young horse's back will be particularly sensitive and it is important to give it adequate protection – a sore back is bound to make him uncomfortable and unco-operative, and he might even have to stop work altogether. I use the Mexican-style saddle cloths under my saddles which are ideal; as well as protecting the horse's back, they are not so bulky that I lose contact with the horse through my seat and legs.

Bits

s e l e c t i n g

40

It is best to be flexible about the sort of bit used on the young horse, but I like to start him off in a snaffle and use a noseband with a drop action if more control is necessary, such as a flash or grakle; these prevent him opening his mouth to resist, and also stop him getting his tongue over the bit which is a difficult habit to correct. It is impossible to generalise as to what the correct bit might be because every horse, young or old, will react in a different way; the correct bit is the one that works! Nevertheless, the whole point of training is that the young horse learns to respond willingly to the rider's aids, and this is infinitely preferable to relying on a severe bit for control. Too sharp a bit action may frighten the young horse and make him even more resistant.

If your horse really develops mouth problems – sets his jaw and refuses to turn, fusses his head about – these always seem to re-appear, usually when the pressure is on in competition, however much he seems to improve at home. Start off with something quite gentle, for example a jointed eggbutt or vulcanite-covered snaffle; and if that does not do the trick and he is too strong, only then try something slightly sharper – better that than pulling and yanking at him to no avail. Many riders will change the horse's bit for the jump-off so as to have more control in order to turn more tightly, but this is really only advisable if the horse is not going to mind the change. Some horses take a while to settle in a different bit, so changing it in the middle of the competition can be quite a risk if the horse has never been taken out in that particular bit before. There is nothing more infuriating than getting into a jump-off, changing the bit so as to improve your chances, only to find that the horse resists more strongly when you go back into the arena.

Gill always makes sure that our tack room is kept neat and tidy; there is nothing more infuriating than rummaging around for hours, trying to find that essential item of tack or equipment, when time is precious. The wooden trunks shown here are ideal for storing (and transporting) items of tack, especially rugs. And I might just add that it is so much better to get the rugs cleaned before they are stored away, rather than putting the task off until the following winter!

Martingales

There are different sorts of martingale available, namely Irish, standing and running martingales. I usually use a running martingale because I feel it helps to guide the horse's head into a better carriage. Some horses will never need martingales which is so much the better; young horses particularly can very quickly learn to use a martingale as a 'prop' and lean on it, staying on their forehand and not learning to balance themselves properly. However, I don't like to see horses throwing their heads up in the air: not only can this injure the rider, it also means that the horse can't possibly be listening to the rider's aids or looking where he is going. Any martingale must be fitted correctly; it should neither restrict the horse, nor cause it pain. It does not perform miracles and will only be effective if the rider is using his seat and legs to give the correct aids.

Draw reins

Draw reins are used by most showjumpers and I use them right from the start of my youngsters' training. *However, if you are not familiar with their use, don't attempt to use them without instruction from an expert.*

Draw reins, also known as running reins, should encourage a lower head carriage and thus oblige the horse to work in a better shape; he is thereby in a better position to listen to the rider's aids and eventually to come 'on the bit'. I always find it better to pull the draw reins through the martingale rings so that their effect is to reinforce the rein aid; otherwise they just create a big arc which encourages the horse to overbend. To be properly effective, draw reins must be fitted and used correctly and should *not* be used to drag the horse's head down between his legs; if he is obliged to carry it as low as this he cannot engage his hind legs and in effect you would be forcing him to work on his forehand. When using draw reins it is therefore even more important to ride from the seat and leg, otherwise the horse will simply lean on the running reins and be heavy on the hand; and they should be fitted so that when the horse's head has come down to the correct position the pressure from the rein slackens off. When the draw reins are taken off it is then not such a big step for the horse to carry himself in a good 'shape', particularly if a running martingale is still used.

Care of tack and equipment

All our saddlery is cleaned after use; clean, supple tack will last longer, and is far less likely to rub the horse and make him sore. Neglected leather will only become brittle and may then break, increasing the chance of accident. Before a competition we check everything over – buckles, straps, stitching on all the horse's equipment – to minimise the risk of anything breaking as we are actually jumping. It is always a good idea to have spare stirrup leathers just in case, likewise spare girth and reins. If tack is wiped over and soaped every time it has been used, tack-cleaning is easy; but if dirt and grease has been allowed to build up and go rock-hard, it can take an age to do!

Cleaning tack regularly may sometimes seem unnecessary but it will save on the tedious business of oiling hard, greasy saddlery

selecting

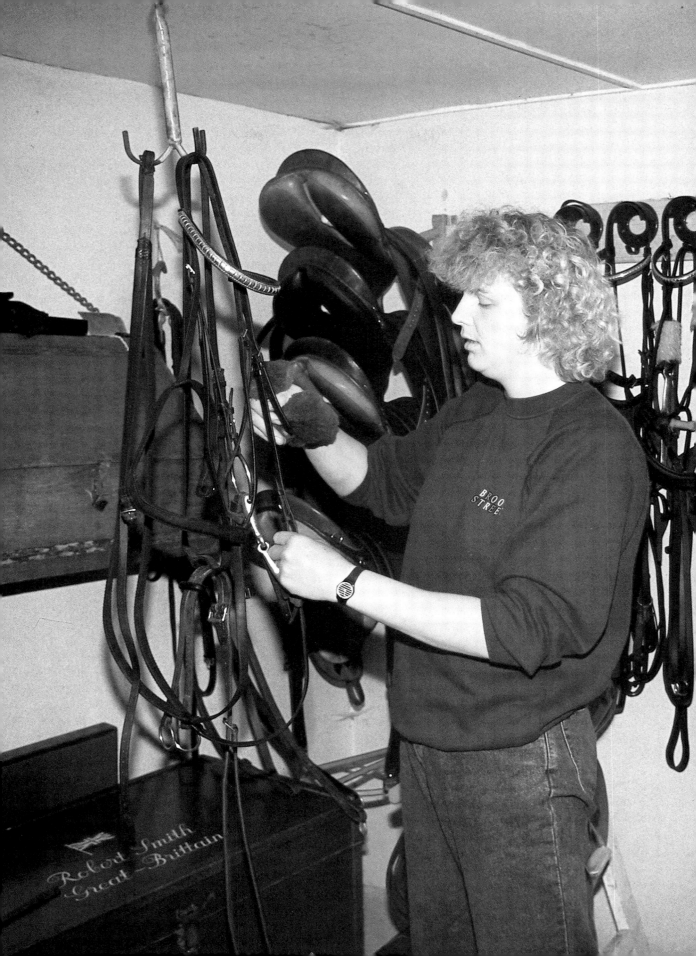

2
TRAINING

When you start training a young horse you are not just teaching him to be obedient, but are starting to build up the muscles he will need to use to an increasingly great extent as he is asked to jump bigger courses. It develops him mentally as well as physically, building up his trust and confidence in his rider, and helping to prevent strains in tendons or muscles through steady fittening work. There can therefore be no short cuts in the training process, and those who try to rush, or leave out any stage of the young horse's early education usually end up regretting their haste, with a youngster that is confused and frightened, to the extent of being totally unco-operative – and who can blame it?

It is difficult to assess the ultimate potential of the unbroken youngster; the talented few will make it to Grade A standard, but although many may become good middle-of-the-road performers, most will never be good enough to get to the top. This is no reason for your average trainer/rider to start off feeling despondent, because such an outlook will never bring positive results; but with the right training any horse can be helped to make the best use of whatever ability it possesses. As for any athlete, most of us can achieve success to a certain standard, even if we are never going to break world records – and should certainly expect to enjoy the sport at whatever level we are capable of competing at. This is a fundamental proviso, and the basis of any training method: that to compete with success, both the rider and the horse must enjoy their work and love jumping; all the hours spent in preparation and riding really should be fun.

Early Training Lessons

training

Getting the basics right

If the young horse is to be expected to work well, it is most important that the schooling area is level and flat, with a good surface. Outside, a nice thick covering of grass is best – on no account should the going be boggy. We use our paddocks in rotation so they can be left to 'rest' in turn; droppings are removed regularly to prevent worm infestation, and we harrow them over about three times a year. All these are measures to keep a decent surface. Of course, all-weather surfaces and indoor schools are ideal, and although not everybody is lucky enough to have one of their own, most people if they are sufficiently determined can get to one if conditions demand it. Otherwise try and find a relatively flat field, and if part of it can be fenced off for schooling in, this is even better because a more enclosed area will help the horse to concentrate. There is nothing more tempting to a youngster than a huge grass field for a good buck around, so let's at least start with a measure of co-operation from the horse! Check that the area of the field you intend to use is free of ruts or potholes, and anything else which could cause unnecessary accidents – old bottles and bits of glass or wire, rubbish or stones. At Quendon we are lucky enough to have an indoor school, but we do jump the horses in the field as well. Sand has been laid down in the field on the approach and landing of the fences to try and minimise jarr as much as is possible to our horses' legs; it is several inches deep to provide adequate 'cushioning' and is regularly raked over to keep it level. This is a small price to pay in comparison to the value of our horses where leg strain or injury may curtail their showjumping career. Not many horses like jumping on hard ground, either, so the less punishment your horse incurs the more he will enjoy his work.

We have laid down sand in one of our fields to provide a good surface on which to school our horses. It is a fairly expensive exercise, but there is no doubt that it is worth it; it greatly reduces jarring on their legs

t r a i n i n g

Early days

Training a young horse is a slow process and it would be quite wrong to expect miracles at the beginning. Just as building up our own muscles and fitness demands a progressive routine, so it does for the horse, too. Gradually strengthening his muscles and suppling his joints will mean that his physical frame will not be overstressed, and will minimise the risk of straining ligaments and muscles. A four-year-old horse is still far from being fully developed, so it is up to the trainer/rider to ensure that the exercise he receives through his training routine is encouraging the development of a good 'jum-ing physique'. I like to see muscle building up over the loins and back-end to give well-shaped, powerful hindquarters, and also over the shoulders; only if he has muscle in the right place will the horse have the impetus to jump well.

The stage at which training starts will obviously depend on how much experience the horse has had. If it is unbroken, there is going to be a lot more time and patient work involved for the trainer, who will need to allow for this. There are different trains of thought concerning breaking in: many like to break in a horse as a three-year-old and then turn it out for another year to grow up and mature; others like to give the horse only a short break; some prefer to keep it in light work with no break at all. Really it depends how mature the horse is. I usually buy somewhat older horses and school them on, because we simply can't afford the time to start horses on a regular basis; nor do we have the room to 'run them on', which means

Handling a horse correctly from the outset is an important and influential part of its training. A bad experience can ruin a horse. A good trainer is essential

the costs of keeping them those extra years are too high. Fortunately all my Grade A horses have been quick learners, which is unusual for Irish horses; continental horses are usually more receptive.

It is essential that the horse has happy memories of handling as this will be the foundation of the trust and confidence we hope to establish between him and his rider. I would suggest that if you do not feel sufficiently knowledgeable to do this yourself, then send the horse to somebody who is, and who is experienced in this first stage of training. Despite the extra cost it is well worth paying, and the horse will certainly benefit in the long term.

 Handling

Young horses under three years old are best left to run in a big open field, with their own companions, and should *not* be over-handled. If they are halter-broken at an early age and just helped to be basically confident with people this makes things easier for the handler later, but they should *not* be fussed and fiddled with. If they are, they will end up being thoroughly cocky and obstinate, and usually much more awkward to break in. Once they are started, by all means handle them sensibly: they must learn to stand tied up, have their feet picked out and rasped by the blacksmith, to be groomed and led about – all in a calm, relaxed manner.

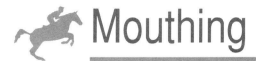

Mouthing

Bits with keys can be used to 'mouth' the horse: the keys help to moisten the mouth and encourage him to play with the bit and accept it, rather than to grasp it with his teeth and take too solid a hold. Some people prefer to use a jointed snaffle to do this, probably either an eggbutt jointed snaffle with cheekpieces, or a vulcanite D-ring jointed snaffle; these are less likely to pull through into the horse's mouth if he is obstinate about turning when being lunged or ridden. Again, this is down to personal choice. Occasionally a youngster may show some resistance to having the bit put in his mouth and the bridle pulled over his ears, but persevere calmly and gently; you can always dismantle the bridle, slip it over his neck and push it quietly forward into position. With practice, the horse will soon become accustomed to having the bit in his mouth and the bridle pulled over his ears, and on no account should he be yanked around at any stage in this process.

I must admit that I have actually broken in very few of the youngsters that come to our yard every year. Anyway, each horse is different from the next, so when I explain what we do I am simply describing a basic method, and there are certainly no hard and fast rules. We play everything by ear and do not rush anything.

Long-reining

If all is going well, the next stage is for the young horse to be taken out on long-reins. Whoever is doing the long-reining needs to be experienced – a handler who is hanging on to the end of the reins and wrapping himself around every other tree is not going to achieve very much at all! Long-reining is an excellent means of teaching the horse to go away from home, and will also help to get him used to sights and sounds outside his field. Driving in long-reins used to be much more popular – nowadays busy roads can make this procedure positively dangerous, though long-reining can still be quite a useful exercise for teaching the horse to behave in light traffic.

When long-reining, you can ask the horse to halt, move forwards, turn and steady, all of which gradually gets him used to the idea of contact from the reins. Always use a breaking roller which has rings to thread the long-reins through: it is pointless hanging on to long-reins that don't stay down on the horse's sides. Breaking rollers can be bought in both leather and webbing. The leather ones are stronger, their only disadvantage being that they feel colder to the horse's back. Also, be sure to keep a leather roller clean and supple so that it doesn't rub and make the horse sore. For long-reining, as for lungeing, it is a good idea for the handler to wear a pair of gloves to help maintain a secure hold on the reins, and shoes with soles that grip well.

Gradually the youngster should become more settled on the long-reins, and will soon be ready to go a stage further. Again, I must stress there can be no time limits, and progress will be very much according to the individual horse.

Lungeing

I have never really been persuaded that a lot of lungeing is a good thing, but must admit that when breaking in a young horse it is a convenient way of accustoming him to carrying a saddle and wearing side-reins. Some people don't like to lunge a horse before the age of three years because of the unnatural stresses put on the back and joints, though I do think it rather depends on the maturity of the horse and is something that can be done in moderation. The side-reins must be of equal length – you will never achieve a better bend by tightening the inside rein; the horse will either resist, or simply turn his head inwards and swing his quarters out. Proper length bend, where the horse's whole body follows the shape of the circle, only comes as the horse gets progressively more supple through a planned sequence of training exercises.

When lungeing, I always make sure the horse is wearing brushing boots on all four legs, and that the schooling surface is even. Young horses should be started on a fairly large circle; as they progress, the circle can be made smaller – but the smaller the circle, the more you are asking them to bend and the greater is the stress put on their joints and muscles. If the horse is going calmly and sensibly on the lunge, then I might ask him to pop over a few small jumps – but I do prefer to see a horse jump with a rider on board, right from the start.

Backing

When the handler feels confident that the horse is quite relaxed in his lessons, then it is probably time for him to be backed and ridden on. If the horse has been handled properly there should be few problems when the rider actually gets on – though there is always the odd one that objects! Backing a horse should only ever be contemplated in an enclosed area with a competent person holding the horse; to attempt it in a large open field is asking for problems! We always lean over a young horse first of all, so he can get used to the extra weight on his back; we will also do this from each side, so as to be quite sure he doesn't object to dangling (human!) legs whichever side they might appear! Encourage him to move a few steps: if he doesn't mind, well and good; if he does, you can just slip off and repeat the exercise next day. The next stage would be to swing your leg over – being very careful not to touch his quarters as you do so, and keeping your own body low on his neck the first time – so you are sitting on him properly. Do not put your feet in the stirrups, and sit *very* still, without making any sudden movements that may startle him. The following day we may ask a little more of the horse, by walking him around quietly; we would do this until he seemed quite settled about carrying the weight of a rider, and it may take several days.

Obviously, breaking in the young horse is a very complex subject and one that can be discussed at great length: these really are the basic guidelines. And I would emphasise once again, that whoever is breaking in the horse *must* be confident and experienced – a nervous rider and a young unbroken horse is the perfect recipe for disaster. As the trust and confidence between horse and rider strengthens, a little trot work can be introduced; but it is vital to keep these work sessions *short* in these early stages – 15 minutes at the most.

Loose schooling
This method can sometimes be effective, and there are many riders who loose school their young horses regularly. They believe that in this way, the horse's introduction to jumping

comes as less of a shock because it only has to find its own balance and can jump at the speed it likes; it doesn't have the rider to worry about as well. However, I hold to my conviction that it is better to get a horse jumping with a rider on its back whenever possible – after all, it will have to learn to do this at some stage in its career. I very rarely loose school my horses, and prefer to get them

accustomed to their surroundings by going out on light hacks in the company of a schoolmaster. This helps to build up their confidence and get them used to traffic and other everyday hazards. When a horse has gained more confidence he can be hacked out alone; take care that he does not become too dependant on another horse or he might become nappy when ridden alone.

Early flatwork

Before we even consider jumping the young horse, it is immensely important to train him thoroughly on the flat, and indeed to continue that training throughout his competitive career as a showjumper. The aim is to have a horse which is easy to manoeuvre because he is supple, light in the hand and so immediately responsive; and as strong and fit as we can get him, so he can make the very best of what jumping ability he possesses.

To begin with, I find it is enough just to walk the horse around and let him get used to his surroundings. Some people prefer to lunge the horse before they get on him, so he can get rid of his excess energy; but I must admit I only lunge a few of our horses. A little lungeing doesn't harm any horse, but some can get dopey and sour if they are lunged too much. Ten minutes of serious lungeing is

equivalent to about two hours' hacking, so it can take a lot out of a horse. It is probably more suitable for those that are very excitable when they are first ridden; in this case it helps to solve a problem, because instead of fighting the rider the horse is just fighting against himself. Ultimately lungeing does help him to relax – but I don't like to fall into the habit of lungeing every day.

I use the horsewalker for all my horses: it provides an excellent way of loosening them up before exercise, and cooling them down after they have been ridden. Fifteen to twenty minutes before they are ridden is usually sufficient to loosen them up well, and saves precious time in a busy yard!

We find the horsewalker invaluable at Quendon. The young Irish mare shown here is walking round quite happily whilst cooling down after exercise

So, we have our youngster in the field: if he has not been on the horsewalker we walk him around for about 20 minutes; if he has, we spend only 5 to 10 minutes in loosening up. Once he is settled in walk, we can ask him to do a bit more. To find out how obedient he is to our aids we do some circles, on both reins, still in walk, and now and again asking him to halt and walk on again. I find the following exercise very effective when trying to establish just *how* supple and responsive the horse is: I bring him back to halt, then ask him to bend his head and neck right round to one side so that he is almost facing my toes; then I ask him to do it to the other side. This helps to relax his spine, and is really the rider's way of saying 'Are you listening to me? Because if you're not, now is the time to start!'. This will become easier as the horse becomes supple.

It is quite common for horses to be more stiff on one side than the other. Always start on the good side and then work on the stiff side when schooling – not necessarily for a longer time, but making sure that he works properly on that rein. Watch a horse when he is loose in the field: very often you will see that when he is cantering around he always sets off on the same leg and maybe always keeps the same bend whichever direction he is going in. It is similar to us being either right- or left-handed – we are generally one or the other, and very few of us are ambidextrous! However, our young horse will to learn to canter with the correct leg – the inside one – leading on turns, otherwise he will find it very difficult to stay sufficiently balanced to jump properly in the tighter confines of the showjumping ring.

The next stage is to do a little basic trot work. Never trot in the same direction all the time, but try to do as much work on one rein as the other. Trot in figures of eight and in a variety of different patterns – serpentines, loops, changes of rein across the diagonal – making sure the horse is between hand and leg so his whole body follows the line, whether it is curved or straight, of each movement. Rising trot is more effective than sitting trot for suppling the young horse, and we must encourage him to find a balanced rhythm and be 'on the bit'. A horse is said to be 'on the bit' when he accepts it willingly

Patricia is settling the mare and is concentrating on work in trot before she progresses on to some jumping. She is working well with the aid of draw reins – notice the slight bend to the inside, and how the mare is engaging her hocks as a result

with his head in the correct position and his hind legs well under him; by applying more pressure with the legs and seatbones the rider can then ask the horse for more activity, or impulsion. He controls this with the hands: when they 'give' a little the horse must learn to go forward, when they close he should lower his head and engage his hindquarters – and according to the degree of leg and closing of the hand the horse will slow down or stop. In this way the forehand becomes lighter and more freely active, since the back end is becoming more engaged and powerful.

Teaching the horse to lengthen and shorten his strides – at first in trot – is a vital part of the showjumper's training because when we jump a course we will be asking the horse to adjust his stride all the time, so as to arrive at the best take-off point, through combination fences, and where two jumps are built with a related distance between them; he must therefore learn to 'come back' to shorten his stride, and 'go on' to lengthen it. This is discussed in more detail in the chapter on More Advanced Training. Use half-halts to improve the youngster's obedience: the half-halt is in effect a signal to him that you want his attention, and you achieve it by closing the legs on the girth and closing the hand momentarily – the horse should relax his jaw, lower his head and engage his hind legs, *without* any deceleration of pace – and as

The rein-back can sometimes be a difficult movement to master on a young horse. This horse is grasping the concept well and stepping back quite calmly

soon as he does this, the rider should open the hand a little, keeping the leg on so the horse goes forward immediately. All this should be achieved over the space of only two or three strides.

I like to use the rein-back frequently throughout the horse's schooling. In this movement the horse must come back onto the bit, it brings him back onto his hocks and makes him use his joints; and again, it is a test of the horse's concentration and obedience. When asking the horse to step backwards the last thing you want is a battle with the horse resisting the aids. He should halt quite squarely; the rider should then close the legs behind the girth as if asking the horse to walk on, but instead of giving with the hand, he keeps it closed – in response to the hands and legs used thus the horse should step backwards. This does take some practice, and on no account pull at the horse; many youngsters are not willing to step backwards to begin with because they do not quite understand what is being asked of them. In this situation, it is useful to have somebody on the ground with a schooling whip to just tap the horse on the front legs, which should encourage him to take a step backwards. When he does so, praise him immediately.

Poles on the ground are an excellent way to establish the horse's rhythm in all three paces. You can start off with just one pole on the ground, so that the youngster can take a look at it, then gradually add poles one by one until you have probably got five or six; for trotting, the poles should be about 4ft 6in (1.4m) apart, for walking they should be closer together, 3ft 6in–4ft (1–1.2m). We do not want the horse to cat-leap over these poles and would probably ask him to walk over them first; in all this early pole work what we are trying to establish are the basic principles of jumping, and the right attitude in the horse – he must learn not to rush, to

stay straight and in an even rhythm, and in all things to listen to his rider. Once he walks over these poles on the ground calmly we can start to trot him over them (making sure they are moved slightly further apart); this sort of work helps to improve the horse's balance and also gets him used to the idea of coloured poles. The next step is to raise the poles a few centimetres off the ground, which will encourage him to flex his joints even more. It is important not to rush the young horse over the poles, but to let him find his own way through a grid. Always make sure you are approaching them straight, too, otherwise you are not giving him a fair chance of finding a nice even stride through the line of poles.

To teach the horse how to balance and use himself on turns and corners, poles can be laid on the ground round a corner of the arena in a fan shape. It is remarkable how often a horse and rider are seen diving round corners like a motorbike, even in the jumping arena! And in a showjumping course, how often is there a jump off a turn? If a horse dives when he turns, he will find it hard to re-balance himself and make a good jump. The rider

![horse logo] This sequence shows me taking the horse through a very simple grid in canter. As we enter, I make sure that he goes to the centre of the poles in the same way as I would approach the middle of a jump. By giving with my hands, I have allowed him to balance himself, but I am also encouraging him through pressure from my legs. He has entered the first part of the grid well and is really using his hocks. All the time I sit still in the saddle letting the horse find his own way out of the grid. He is using himself so well here that he decides to jump out over the last section! There is a good rounded outline, and you can see how the horse becomes lighter in front the more he moves his hocks under his body

training

must give the horse all the assistance he can to help him stay balanced, and to do this the horse must learn right from the start to listen to the rider's leg and move away from it. The aim is to 'hold' the horse between the inside leg and outside hand – in other words, use your inside leg to push him into the outside rein; in this way the horse will learn to balance himself and not 'fall in' as he turns, and this is essential for jumping courses.

Always attempt the grid from both directions, and vary the work with occasional circles and changes of pace so the horse never quite knows what he has to do next. In this way the work will not become monotonous – it is equally important to keep the horse happy and enthusiastic in his lessons. It is all a good test of obedience, too; each jumping course is going to be different and this should not be forgotten in our schooling.

 # Canter work

Once I am satisfied with the way a young horse is going in trot, I like to try a little canter work. Canter work on each leg is a very good way to build muscle and improve balance, but should only be for short spells at this stage because the young horse is probably not all that strong and fit, and exhausting him will not teach him anything. Cantering on the correct lead may take some practice and a horse will nearly always find it easier to strike off on one leg than on the other. Wait until you get to a corner, then place your weight to the inside, with the outside leg behind the girth to 'lift' the horse

onto the correct leg. Never let a horse canter round on the wrong leg.

At this stage the canter should not be too slow or 'collected'; the horse must carry himself and not rush off, but if you slow him too much in the early stages he will learn to lean and pull. Practise coming back from canter to trot to halt – not pulling at him, but by just sitting up and 'holding' with the hand – and as this exercise improves, coming back from canter straight to halt; then try from halt into canter. All this will take some time but soon the horse's confidence will increase, and more can be asked of him.

Basic Education

Showing the use of a 'channel' to guide the horse
to the centre of the jump

Once the young horse has successfully understood all these initial exercises, and is working calmly and confidently on the flat and over our poles on the ground, we can ask him to tackle something a little bit more demanding. Do remember however, that when schooling the youngster it is vital to be sure that he is fit enough in his body and mature enough in his mind to cope with what is being asked of him. The whole concept of jumping and schooling is probably fairly new to him and he will be burning up a great deal of energy through the unaccustomed physical effort, perhaps excitement and even nervous energy, particularly if he is highly strung. I like all my young horses to go out on regular hacks; this helps to relax them, but also keeps them on their toes and interested in life. It is an important part of their education for them to get used to strange surroundings – they will have to cope with plenty of very unfamiliar sights and sounds when they go to their first show – so I like them to learn to settle down in the 'world outside the arena' very early on. The larger shows usually have amusements for children, a favourite being the 'bouncy castle' – totally mind-blowing to our young horse!

At home I might therefore school the young horse for half-an-hour, then take him for half-an-hour's hack to let him unwind and relax. A happy horse is always far more willing to please than a bored, dejected one who will rapidly lose enthusiasm for his work and for life in general. And it is amazing how differently the horse will behave when you actually take him to his first show. He will certainly be excited because it is all so new to him – but at least we can be sure that it *is* only excitement, and not because he is afraid of all the traffic and people on a showground.

Gridwork

Gridwork is an excellent way to train the young horse and to keep him fit and athletic throughout his competitive life, as all grids can be built according to the horse's ability. I do a lot of this sort of work with my novices because it is an effective way of introducing them to combinations; if they are well schooled through grids, jumping one fence straight after another in the showjumping ring does not then come as such a shock to them. I never make grids too big because they are not supposed to test how high the horse can jump: they are to teach him to approach his fences and jump them *without* changing his rhythm; to jump in a nice shape with rounded back and good bascule; to stay straight; and to tuck his legs up neatly as he jumps.

If the young horse has managed our raised trotting poles successfully, or maybe a pole on the ground and 9ft(2.7m) to a small cross-pole fence, he should be quite ready to do a bit more. Most horses seem to enjoy doing simple grids, and at this stage the rider should interfere as little as possible so as to allow the horse full freedom of his head and neck; in this way he will learn to look at what he is doing and think for himself, and find his own balance. So from the pole on the ground to the cross-pole 9ft(2.7m) away we can introduce a second cross-pole fence say at a bounce distance (10–12ft/3–6m), and gradually build up the grid with more small jumps; for example one stride to a cross-pole and rail (18ft/5.4m), then another stride to a small square parallel (21ft/6.3m) – or you could add two strides (34ft/10.2m) to, say, an upright. Cross-fences encourage horses to go over the centre of a jump and not to hug the wings; they are inviting, and grids built in this way help to build up the horse's confidence and his trust in the rider. The distances between jumps in a grid can be pulled out or closed up slightly so the horse has to take a longer or a shorter stride between them; if the distances are short it encourages him to snap up his front legs more quickly and be rounder in his jump – slightly longer, and he learns to go forward from the rider's leg. However, at this stage the variation should really only be very small – 6in (15cm) would probably be enough.

If a horse is lazy or careless and 'dangles' his front legs, or if he tends to drift left or right as he jumps, it is a good idea to rest a pole on each side of a jump: this provides a 'channel' and will keep the horse straight as he jumps; it will also dissuade him from taking a side exit. It is always easier to prevent a problem than to correct one!

This shows an ideal grid to approach in trot. The pole in front of the cross pole is there to steady the mare and to encourage her to find a good stride for take-off

I like to combine all gridwork with the horse's routine exercises on the flat; I might circle before and afterwards, and if the horse is really calm and relaxed, I will maybe practise coming in on each leg in canter. Remember however, if attempting a grid in canter, it is vital to lengthen the distance between the fences – the average trot stride is 9ft(2.7m) and an average canter stride is 12ft(3.6m). And if there is the least sign of rushing or excitability, then you must go back to trot; incorporating half-halts and rein-back helps to get the horse's attention if he does start to feel over-zealous about the idea. Although it may seem tedious to keep going back over basics it is really the only way to achieve good results. So to reiterate, what are we hoping to achieve at this stage? In short:

general obedience to the rider's aids;
suppling the horse's muscles and joints;
improving the horse's confidence;
encouraging the horse to think for itself;
maintaining a balanced rhythm;
increasing the engagement of the hocks.

As we persevere calmly and methodically with the youngster's training on the flat, after a while we should see a marked improvement. However, it is impossible to say how quickly any one horse will progress in the training programme we have devised for him – some horses take much longer than others to accomplish their lessons. Patience is of the essence: building up confidence can be a very slow process, and we must be extremely careful that the horse continues to enjoy his jumping. A good rider will do everything possible to make these early lessons a pleasurable experience for the horse: he will be very sympathetic with the hands so as never to yank the horse's mouth, and will do all he can not to bump back into the saddle as the horse lands on the other side of a fence. Horses have very sensitive backs, and particularly when they are young when their muscles have not had a chance to develop to their full strength. It is easier to keep in balance with the horse when he is cantering and jumping if your weight is more forward

so that your knee-joints are absorbing the movement; to this end, shorten your stirrups at least two holes – enough to bring your seat out of the saddle, whilst keeping a secure contact with your leg. If your stirrups are too long, your lower leg will tend to swing forward and you *will* bump up and down on his back. Although the rider should be giving aids which are clear to the horse, this does *not* mean that legs and arms should be flapping about; untidy riding is more likely to confuse him. It is discreet and gentle pressure from the legs, seatbones and hands that is the most effective. My own view is that if a rider is not sufficiently competent or experienced, then he or she should not consider schooling a young horse – it is the perfect recipe for disaster.

Increasing collection

As the horse becomes more supple, the movements we can ask of him on the flat which he should be able to achieve can be more advanced, and as he copes with the work more easily and becomes lighter to ride, the nearer he is coming towards true collection. To reiterate, this is the lowering of the hindquarters and generating of more energy in the horse's back end as the hocks move under his bodyweight, resulting in his front end becoming correspondingly lighter and more free; the horse feels lighter in the hand – doesn't lean or pull – and altogether easier to manoeuvre. He has a nice rounded outline – his back is not hollow – and has a reasonable degree of flexion at the poll (carries his head near to the vertical – but with a 'lifted', freer shoulder and front end).

To lower the head and engage the quarters, the first step towards collection, the rider must apply pressure with the legs and seatbones together with a supporting contact from the reins (as for the half-halt). This all sounds suspiciously like dressage, and

The mare is beginning to enjoy herself and is taking quite a pull. Patricia sits deeply into the saddle and is using her outside leg and inside hand to guide the mare back into a more 'collected' shape

Above: The trotting poles have really made this horse use his hocks instead of dragging himself along on his forehand. He is adopting a much more pronouced knee and hock action

Right: Suppling exercises are an essential part of the showjumper's training and will improve the horse's agility and style. The important consideration is not to expect instant miracles – it does require patience!

essentially it is. However, it is all relevant to our showjumper's training because we need to generate as much activity and impulsion as possible from the horse's back end so he can power over the jumps. The greater the height and width of the fence, the higher the degree of collection we require from the horse, in order to have enough bunched-up power and energy to jump a big fence cleanly.

Leg yielding

This teaches the lateral aids – hand and leg on the same side – and in response the horse learns to yield to the pressure of the rider's leg. In effect this exercise helps him to stay balanced on turns, and increases his suppleness. It is best to start in walk. The horse must stay quite straight in his body, but the head is slightly turned away from the direction you want to go; the horse moves on four tracks. For example, apply your right leg one hand behind the girth: the horse's quarters should move half a step to the left; your left leg is positioned on the girth to

encourage the horse to keep moving forwards. The right hand keeps a firm contact to bring the horse's head slightly to the right; the left hand simply dictates the degree of bend wanted. The horse should stay straight in his body. This exercise can be performed with left leg behind the girth and firm left hand, moving the quarters to the right. As the youngster gets more compliant, you can ask for more steps like this and then try it in trot.

Shoulder-in

This is a useful suppling exercise where the horse moves on three tracks with great emphasis on length bend (bend through the length of his body); done correctly, the hind

leg steps under the body more and the horse carries himself more 'from behind', thus becoming more 'collected'. For example, the horse is asked to bend its head and neck to the inside, and the inside leg is applied one hand behind the girth; the outside hand and outside leg help to keep the horse's length bend and prevent the shoulders and quarters from escaping outwards. In effect the horse moves forwards in a straight line but on three tracks because his body is bent as if he were on a circle. Shoulder-in therefore helps to establish the horse's length bend, and strengthens the hindquarters as it demands greater flexion in the joints in the hindlegs. In consequence, the shoulders become lighter so a freer movement is encouraged. The young horse will find it very difficult to sustain the increased effort this exercise demands, so we should only do it for short periods at a time; he will almost certainly try to evade the movement when we first attempt it, in which case ride a circle to re-establish rhythm and back-leg activity, and try again as you come off the circle.

Flying changes

In the showjumping arena the horse must be able to change his leading leg easily and quickly in canter should he need to turn and balance himself quickly in order to jump. To perform a 'flying change' is in fact quite an advanced and difficult movement, but it is something I like to teach my young horses as soon as possible. The rider must be quite experienced to do this properly and must understand the horse's footfall sequence in canter, and the horse must understand thoroughly the aids to canter, otherwise he may change legs in front but not behind, becoming 'disunited' and unbalanced. In canter with the near-fore leading the sequence is this: off-hind pushes the horse into movement; then right diagonal of off-fore and near-hind follows; then near-fore. Then follows a moment of suspension when all four feet are off the ground. To ask the horse for a flying change, I establish a nice rhythmic canter, bring him to attention by using a half halt on a circle, then at the moment of suspension, *reverse* the aids to canter for that leg, so that my outside leg comes forward and my inside leg moves back, slightly behind the girth. If everything goes well (and it probably won't at first!), then the horse will change legs in the air and continue in canter on the other lead immediately.

It is important that the rider does not rush the horse into this exercise because the horse will risk becoming too hollow – there needs to be a lot of collection. However, if the horse cannot manage a flying change in the arena, then we won't stand much chance of clearing a fence off a turn, so it is something I like to master at home when preparing for a show.

 ## The first proper jumps

Now we have established a reasonable degree of suppleness and obedience in the horse, we can think about jumping proper fences – it is a great feeling of progression! I never attempt anything too taxing at this stage and would start with a simple small upright. Depending how sensibly the horse is going at the time, I might put a couple of poles on the ground to trot over to help him regulate his stride as he approaches the fence. I would also place my two 'guiding' poles on each side of the fence, forming the channel to encourage the horse to go straight through. I am a great believer in using canter poles for a young horse too, because they help him a great deal in steadying and regulating his approach; if his approach to a fence is wrong – rushed or excited, even too slow – there is no way he will be able to jump well. Also, remember that whereas the rider looks at the top pole of the fence to judge the height, the horse looks at the bottom for a groundline and then measures upwards. Therefore, to make it easy for a young horse, I always place a pole on the ground but push it out a short distance from the jump, to make it easier for the horse to measure it correctly. Incidentally, it is never a good idea to use white poles in the early stages because horses have difficulty in seeing them. Make everything as easy as you possibly can for the youngster during his introduction to practice fences.

The following is a synopsis of what the horse actually does as he jumps, and what the rider should do in order to stay with the movement and help the horse to jump to the best of his ability.

The approach

As the horse approaches a fence he will instinctively lower his head in order to measure it and judge his take-off point; it is therefore most important that his rider allows him to do this. As such, I will bring the horse in straight at a steady rhythmic pace, thus giving him every chance of seeing the fence clearly. I keep my slightly forward position in the saddle, and by maintaining a quiet but steady pressure with my legs and a light but steady, even contact through the reins, I ask the horse to keep a more 'collected' outline, thus preventing him (or doing my best to prevent him!) from hollowing his back and raising his head in the air. All the time I am keeping the power and energy in the horse's back legs and not letting him tip onto his forehand, but at the same time being very careful *not* to pull him back with my hands. A few metres from take-off, I go with the horse's movement, but maintain and probably increase the pressure with my seat and legs so that it is quite clear to the horse that I definitely intend him to clear the jump; it is up to me to give him confidence, to make him 'think forward', because he will sense if I am slightly half-hearted and then we are half-way to a refusal: *not* what is wanted, at *any* stage of training!

If we are to stand a fair chance of clearing a jump then the approach must be perfect (or as near perfect as possible!). Both horse and rider must be looking at and concentrating on the jump, approaching on a central and straight line. Here I am at 'take off' point at a practice fence at Hickstead

Many riders complain they cannot 'see' a stride. The best way to teach yourself this is to practise over small fences, then if you do make mistakes it won't really matter. Establish the horse's canter in a nice even rhythm, then approach the fence within that rhythm, not changing the pace in any way: if you do have to adjust the horse's stride, always go for a shorter stride – in this way the horse will learn to round his back and tuck up his front legs; if you kick for a 'long one', he will learn to jump flat and be less careful with his legs. You should *never* hold the horse up tight and bounce on the spot while you look for the right stride, and then when you do see it, launch him at the jump like a catapult. He will find it almost impossible to 'round' himself and bascule if he is ridden in this way. Keep the shape and the rhythm, and adjust within that rhythm.

The take-off

The grids used in these early stages of the horse's training should have taught him to measure a fence and define where to take off. At the moment of take-off my horse will need to carry his head and neck low: if they are too high at this point – if I am flustering the horse in any way with too sharp a hand – he will find it difficult to bring his hocks right underneath his body so as to lift his forehand off the ground. He will not need to stretch himself too far over a small jump, but I will still make quite sure that I allow him full freedom of his head and neck so he can stretch them low over the jump; in flight he must learn to use head and neck like this so as to bascule to the best of his ability – only in this way can he *really* fold up his legs and tuck away his feet, and clear the big fences without touching a pole.

...and we have lift off! Look how the horse has tucked up his front legs and how my weight is just going with the movement, that is not too far forward or, worse still, too far back. I am giving with the reins so as not to interfere with the horse's natural movement or balance in any way

t
r
a
i
n
i
n
g

The landing

As the horse lands it is vital to 'go with him' – not to get 'left behind' otherwise we will land with a smack onto the back of the saddle (his loins); and equally, not to get pitched forward onto his shoulder (usually because we are looking down, and our head – which is heavy! – is in front of the horse's centre of balance) which will make it very hard for the horse to re-balance himself before the next jump is upon him. Sometimes holding onto a neck strap is a good idea if in the early stages the horse is trying to cat-leap. As he lands, his head and neck will come up; first one foreleg will touch the ground, then the other, and the hind legs will then come through to take the bodyweight. I then like the horse to move away with power and impulsion, though by this I do not mean him to gallop off into the horizon! It is up to the rider to gather the horse up after a jump; he might say to the horse 'I've given you the freedom to go over the jump, now come back to me'.

It is often a good idea to place a canter pole on the landing side of a fence so the horse 'takes a check' once he has landed; it is an effective way of steadying him, and so also helps the rider collect him again in preparation for the next fence.

This photograph illustrates the enormous pressure placed on the fetlock joints on landing as the first foot down has to withstand the horse's weight. The horse's back has straightened out and I help him by sitting as quietly as possible, maintaining a gentle contact; getting left behind and coming down with a 'thud' on the saddle is enough to put him off jumping for life, and can cause ligament problems, not to mention a sore back

*t
r
a
i
n
i
n
g*

As the horse becomes more confident we can gradually introduce a variety of different fences and eventually make up a small course. By including spreads and uprights, parallels and hog's back type fences, the horse learns to adapt himself to various widths and heights. Help him as much as possible in the early stages by making a definite groundline in front of each jump. It is the rider's responsibility to guide the horse in straight, and to 'see a stride' as well as he can, to help the horse take off in the right place. I never rush the horse in any way because that will only encourage him to jump flat. So often you see riders kicking and racing towards their fences, and it is hardly surprising their horses jump in a style which knocks every other top pole to the ground. Let the fence come to you, rather than you attack the fence.

Different types of jump will need different riding; for example an upright, or a square upright parallel, will need much greater

accuracy in judging where to take off, because the horse must be neat in front to clear the top, or front rail. And the higher the upright, the more collected the horse will have to be, to achieve enough energy and bascule to clear it. Uprights can be made much more inviting if they have brush or some sort of filler in front.

A spread or parallel will need more pace and speed, and a square or box parallel requires a

Left: Introducing different types of fences will add variety to schooling as well as getting the youngster more accustomed to all the 'weird and wonderful' creations he will be confronted with in the showjumping arena. This swing gate stands about 3ft 6in(1.05m) and is a suitable height for schooling purposes

Below: Even experienced horses benefit from going back to basics occasionally, and a simple grid is ideal for ironing out minor problems. Too many riders seem to think they are losing face if they have to lower the jumps, but if they cannot perfect their technique over small fences, they do not stand a chance over the larger, more advanced courses. There is no point in getting over-ambitious with youngsters; more often than not they will lose confidence, and that is far more complicated to put right

greater deal of accurate riding; the horse needs to be collected enough to fire itself in the air and bascule as he would over an upright. An ascending spread such as a triple bar is an inviting fence on the whole, and requires less effort from the horse as there is no upright front rail requiring him to snap up his front legs. However, spread fences should not be made too wide and formidable for the young horse to start with; if he stands off too far he will at best take the back rail, and at worst land in the middle of the fence – neither of which will do very much either for his education or his confidence.

It is important that the stride distances in combinations and related fences are suitable for the horse – even the best will make mistakes if the distances are difficult for them. Horses are not as clever as ponies and very few are capable of 'fiddling' to get you out of trouble! A comfortable distance for a horse to take one non-jumping stride at a slow speed is 24ft (7.40m) and two non-jumping strides would be about 34ft (10.2m); however, these distances will vary according to the horse's natural length of stride, and the going. At this stage we will set up our jumps to suit the horse; quite soon, however, he must learn to adapt his stride to a given distance between fences — this will be discussed in the next section.

At a later stage in training we can introduce water fences and ditches; however, we do not run before we can walk!

Left: Planks look quite inviting but they can prove to be real 'bogey' fences; care must be taken not to take off too far out, causing the horse to jump flat and catch a leg. The take off must be exact

Above: We are really flying over this small spread fence! This is another fence that looks inviting, but in reality the white poles are really quite dazzling and can be difficult for the horse to judge

A variation on the standard practice fence and one that is slightly more intimidating to a youngster. To begin with the horse may be inclined to look down into the ditch so the rider needs to adopt a forceful and positive approach. You may well be faced with this type of fence in an advanced competition, for example the Devil's Dyke at Hickstead

![training horse icon] The rider is trotting the horse towards the jump, which has a pole positioned a short distance away on the approach. The mare trots over the pole then immediately takes off over the small spread. The rider has sat forward in her saddle to let the mare have her head, and judging by the horse's ears, she is not quite settled. However, the rider has used ler legs and the mare immediately takes off and clears the jump well. All the time

![training horse icon] This time, the rider attempts a small upright, again with poles before and after the jump. The mare is jumping better over the upright than the spread – in fact she cleared it by a couple of feet! The pole in front of the jump has encouraged the horse to get deeper into the fence and she has really tucked her front feet in well. On the landing side, the rider has been slightly left behind, but notice how the canter pole is immediately steadying the

the horse is looking straight ahead and concentrating on what she is doing. The pole has helped her to find the correct stride and makes her take a 'check' before going over the jump, and has encouraged the mare to get her

hocks under her, so giving her height over the jump.

Another pole is placed after the jump so, as the mare lands, she again takes a check and it helps the rider to gather her up again in preparation for the next fence

horse. The rider is then given time to regain control and collection, and the mare learns that she cannot gallop off after she has jumped the fence. It is important to understand how the horse uses itself when jumping, and

we must learn to appreciate how valuable gridwork is in suppling muscles and flexing joints. The mare really looks as though she is enjoying herself and this is the basis of building up confidence between horse and rider

More Advanced Training

Introducing a variety of different jumps
is important

training

At this stage I like to see my young horses starting to show positive signs of fitness and health – this is the first chapter in the transformation of the gawky, unco-ordinated, unprepossessing youngster to the beautiful, smoothly athletic jumping machine! By now, the horse's coat should have a deep healthy shine indicating his feeling of well-being both inside and out; the eyes should be bright, and his general demeanour keen and alert; and the muscles in his neck and forearm, over his loins and quarters and in his second thigh should be toning up well, giving that powerful appearance of the true jumping horse. Too many people confuse fat with muscle and it is important that we know exactly what we are looking for: excess fat is carried on the shoulder and over the rib-cage, and where the tail joins the quarters; nor, in a fat horse, will you see that clear definition of the muscle-bands in the neck and quarters typical of a fit horse. A fat horse will never be a fit horse, and it is essential that any horse is fit enough to cope with the level of competition we are aiming him for; otherwise he will not be *able* to give of his best, and we risk damage to back and legs. Some horses appear thick in the wind, and this may indicate that they have too much fat around the lungs – those that start off very fat often retain fat *inside* their body even when they appear to have lost sufficient weight elsewhere (ie on the outside). So, we must feed and exercise our novices to produce muscle and lose excess fat, and maybe give more canter work to those horses entered for longer courses. The horse's back and frame should now be really quite supple, his muscles will be building up thus increasing his 'gymnastic' capabilities, and his daily flatwork exercise will make him increasingly athletic, gradually turning him into that agile jumping horse we so very much desire him to be!

Stamina is really only achieved through a steadily increasing programme of road work, with the occasional canter or faster pipe-opener, preferably slightly uphill to be effective. The actual fitness work must be built up very slowly, and if possible should avoid anything which might cause drama and excitement, particularly with our young horse. Certainly a good canter is a great way to clear the lungs and will also help to muscle up the hindquarters and strengthen the hocks; but we are not training for the Grand National, so any canter work should be conducted at a controlled pace, with the horse working on the bit and in obedience to his rider. Fitness is one of the hardest things to assess, particularly when bringing a horse from the just-broken-in stage to one where his frame – and his confidence – can manage a 'proper' BSJA competition. Moreover just to school him will not necessarily make him *fit* enough in wind and limb to jump for a season in competition. It is generally accepted that roadwork is the best way to harden up a horse's legs; when a young horse or a novice comes up from the field he should walk – briskly, not just slopping along – for about 2 weeks, and older horses usually for longer because ultimately they need to be fitter and their legs harder. If you are conscientious about this, your horse should be less susceptible to muscle and tendon strains later on. However, too much trotting on the road will only cause jarring and so do harm.

On the other hand, any work uphill can only do good because the horse has to work quite hard without covering many miles, which obviously saves wear and tear on legs; it also makes him blow and so improves lung capacity and therefore stamina. If you are working towards BSJA Newcomers or Foxhunter classes the horse should be doing, say 1½ hours of mixed work (schooling and hacking) a day; however, if he is puffing and blowing after only 20 mins schooling on the flat then he is probably not fit enough to jump

An excellent example of a fit young horse enjoying his training. Showjumping requires fitness and agility which is achieved through suppling exercises such as these

training

his way round even a Newcomers' course and will need more *fitness* work (rather than schooling). If you compete with him before he is sufficiently fit he will be more likely to make mistakes, won't be liking it by the time he has finished his round, and may be put off the idea of competitive jumping altogether.

Good ground to work on when cantering and jumping is absolutely essential, since to use bad or uneven ground is the surest way to cause a horse to strain himself somewhere or cut into himself. It should be level, not deep or boggy, without rabbit holes or runs to wear the surface, and without the dreadful unevenness caused by poaching from cattle or horses in wet conditions; ideally it should be firm enough so that it doesn't cut up when the horses work on it, but soft enough to take up some of the concussion – if the footprints you leave are about $1/2$–1in deep, the going is just about right! In bad winter weather, or when the going in summer has got intolerably hard you might lay down sand on each side of your schooling fences as we do at Quendon; and for cantering, racehorse trainers will nearly always hire out their gallops. However, a good grass surface, and for choice old turf, must always be the best to work on.

It is worth stressing again just how impor-tant it is to work out a varied and interesting programme in the training of a young horse; and only by finding out the correct balance of schooling and exercise for each horse will he become fitter and benefit fully from his educa-tion. Hacking out and fittening work give plenty of opportunity to further his general experience, too; quite apart from learning about people and traffic when he goes out on the roads, he must learn about opening and shutting gates when he is ridden over tracks and farmland, and to cope with undulating ground and different going. Hacking out must also be considered as a 'reward' after the horse has been schooled – he should be allowed to relax and just enjoy himself as much as possible. It is a great mistake to jump and jump a horse; it will make him stale and careless, and too many riders do this, failing to leave that little bit extra in the tank to ensure a good ring performance. Schooling indoors all the time can also have this effect, and doesn't do much by way of broadening the horse's education; if he is never taken out and about and exposed to other horses and different environments, he will be so shocked at seeing the big wide world when finally he *is* taken out, that there is very little likelihood of him actually jumping well.

TYPICAL WEEK'S ROUTINE FOR A NOVICE HORSE IN TRAINING
(Routine can be changed depending on day of competition.)

MONDAY	Rest Day	**THURSDAY**	20mins on horsewalker 5–10mins walking on flat 5–10mins trotting exercises – simple grids 15–20mins jumping grids/courses 30mins relaxing hacking

TUESDAY	20mins on horsewalker
	5–10mins walking on flat
	5–10mins trotting exercises –
	  simple grids
	15–20mins jumping grids/
	  courses
	30mins relaxing hacking		

		FRIDAY	30mins horsewalker 30mins hacking
WEDNESDAY	20mins on horsewalker 5–10mins walking on flat 20mins dressage training – small grids 30mins relaxing hacking	**SATURDAY**	Competition
		SUNDAY	30mins horsewalker 30mins flatwork *(May be a rest day if horse has a taxing day when competing.)*

t r a i n i n g

Further flatwork

Our competition horse's schooling on the flat will continue throughout his career, and we will always be seeking to improve his way of going whatever his standard or age. Even the Grade A horses such as Silver Dust and Clover will be worked for a good half-an-hour on the flat before they are jumped at all; it is a way of saying 'listen to me', and also of finding out just how a horse is going on that particular day. Furthermore, my horses would also have been on the horsewalker for about fifteen to twenty minutes beforehand. Exactly how much warming-up work I do depends on the temperament and the fitness of the horse; for example a young horse that is quick and athletic and tends to be excitable is much more likely to be co-operative if it has had the edge taken off its exuberance and is slightly tired. An excited horse will not be very receptive so I will ride him quietly and steadily until he has worked off his excess

energy and is 'listening' to me before I ask anything more complicated. However, be careful not to overdo this working in, particularly with a youngster and above all with an excitable one — he still won't have the stamina to work for long periods of time, and if he is exhausted, or sweated up and in a frenzy he will never feel inclined to listen to his rider but rather will be put off jumping for life! So go slowly; if he takes longer to settle than you expected you may end up doing far less than you had planned in your schooling session, but it is far better to stop *before* he is tired out than to overdo things and risk muscle damage and mental upset.

Whatever the standard of the horse I am riding, I will start by riding him in circles on each rein, using my legs and seat to ask for

The head carriage has become too low and I am using my legs to push him out from this

It is essential to work the youngster on both legs. Most horses are naturally more 'stiff' on one side

bend, collection and obedience before I even think about asking him to jump. A young horse will nearly always tend to be rather on the forehand and therefore lacking engagement from the hindquarters and hocks, so for him, working in on the flat is particularly important; he will not be able to jump at all well until he is 'working from behind', that is, better engaged and lighter in front – only then can he properly 'bascule'. So just as we did in the very first schooling lessons, I might ask the horse to halt and to step backwards so he is bringing his hocks underneath him, then to move forwards again immediately; I will probably trot over a few poles on the ground to regulate the rhythm and length of his stride. This is all absolutely basic 'first lesson' work, but if the horse's way of going is not correct right from the beginning – if we fail to insist on proper rhythm, bend, shape and obedience – then our chances of jumping clear rounds and winning competitions will be greatly reduced. The rider who is conscientious and insists on the 'right way' of doing things – even at the

cost of it taking much longer – is bound to be more successful in the long run than the rider who doesn't bother with a proper training programme in his haste to progress. This could explain why in Britain there are so many 'average' horses and riders, and then such a huge gap in knowledge, experience and ability between these and the dedicated few at the top of the scale.

So now we are asking the youngster for a little bit more in his daily training session, to achieve more collection and greater activity in both the front and back legs. When using draw reins, be particularly careful that the horse doesn't become overbent, because this would be defeating your objective – all the horse is doing then is bending his neck and coming onto his forehand, in fact doing all he can to avoid using his back end with energy and impulsion. I like to spend some time on lateral work, using leg-yielding and shoulder-in to make sure the horse is responsive to my leg, to increase his degree of suppleness and thereby develop this collection. Cantering a figure of eight is another useful exercise at this stage; you can ask for a bit more bend, and it is a movement in which you can establish and practise the flying change. In the showjumping arena the horse will be continually changing direction so it is important that he learns to do this canter change quickly and easily, without becoming disunited or unbalanced. Place a pole on the ground on the imaginary 'interlinking point' of the two circles which form the figure of eight: this will help the horse to understand what we want him to do, at the moment of asking; once he has grasped what is expected of him and changes correctly as soon as we give him the aids, the pole can be taken away.

Practise lengthening and shortening the stride: this is an excellent preparation for related distances, but must be performed correctly in order to be of any use at all – the stride must *lengthen,* first of all, and not simply become more hurried. If the horse persists in 'running', check your riding position – that your leg aids are applied with equal pressure, your back is strong and straight (*not* tipped forward), your hands steady. Always keep to

As the horse becomes more supple we can ask him to work in smaller circles which in turn require more flexibility from the spine

10-metre circle: keep the rhythm – half-halt – strong, equal leg and firm, steady hand; this time, though, you will need even stronger leg aids to drive the hind legs even further under the body. Your hand prevents him from going faster, and so his quarters lower, he raises his forehand and his stride becomes shorter and more elevated.

This is the sort of response you will want from your horse when you ride through a big combination and need to alter the length of his stride: immediate understanding, full of energy, maintaining full power from his quarters and back legs.

In all these exercises the same rhythm must be maintained; it is the first and foremost way of teaching the horse *not* to rush his fences, and to alter his stride *without hurrying*. They will all gradually become easier for the horse to perform; and the stronger his loins and back legs become, the better his jump will be. From time to time it is a good idea for a knowledgeable person to take a good look at the horse from 'on the ground', and to comment on his way of going.

the same procedure when asking for lengthened strides: for example, start in ordinary trot, then give the horse a half-halt to call him to attention, and with driving leg aid and firm but steady contact with the hands, ask him for a more energetic trot on a 10-metre circle; as you emerge from the circle, straighten out either to change the rein across the diagonal or down the long side, and ask him to lengthen: keep steady contact with the reins, maybe lowering and widening them a bit to keep him straight, then push him forwards with the legs just behind the girth and seat bones firmly into the saddle – then use rising trot. He should immediately lengthen, though allow him only a few strides of increase to start with; in the early stages he will find it quite hard to stay balanced and will resort to running again if you ask too much. The whole procedure is as if you were opening and closing the throttle of a car – full of energy and forward movement.

To shorten his stride, ask in the same way as you would ask for the energetic trot on the

The horse is looking far more settled and is responding well to my aids

Gymnastic jumping

The horse should now be ready to manage more demanding grids which are bigger and require more agility and effort on his part. This sort of gymnastic exercise will help to make him more clever when he tackles a course of jumps, and will increase his fitness. A grid that I might well use would be a trotting pole, 9ft(2.7m) to a cross-pole, then 20ft(6m) (one stride) to an upright, and then 34ft(10.2m) (two strides) to a parallel; I can then build on this until I have about six or seven fences in a line, with one or two strides in between. If you like you can reduce the distance a little between the jumps so that the horse learns to shorten himself and to become a bit rounder as he jumps. Height is not important, but the rhythm and the way of jumping is: keep the rhythm even, keep the jumping 'shape' round! I do not build grids any bigger than 3ft 9in, even for my Grade As. I like to use canter poles to encourage the horse to move evenly towards the jumps, and I also use them on the landing side to help him get back into a nice rhythm. I may incorporate several grids into a jumping course.

This sort of gymnastic jumping helps to keep the horse sharp and encourages him to react quickly; grids are also an excellent introduction to doubles and trebles because they teach the horse to jump, think, and then jump again without panicking about his striding. Jumping 'exercises' can also be used to help a horse that is careless; to improve a horse that has a poor natural technique; and to try and correct a bad habit. For example, if a horse is a 'dangler' – one that doesn't tuck up his front legs enough at an upright fence – try placing a low cross-rail in front of an oxer fence; gradually make the back rail higher and move it out, and the horse will have to pick up his shoulder and forearm as it gets bigger. Or, put a pole on the ground about 2ft(60cm) away from the base of an upright; this helps the horse, and particularly the youngster, to judge the correct take-off point and usually encourages him to snap up his front end more promptly.

A horse that keeps knocking down an oxer can sometimes be persuaded to be more careful if you place a rail diagonally from one of the front corners to the opposite back corner; the jump then looks different, and usually the horse will make more effort over it.

Some horses are difficult to keep straight, particularly through a line of fences; always aim for the centre of a fence, and using cross-poles helps the horse to keep to the middle. Two poles placed so that one end rests on the front rail of the fence, the other end on the ground thus making a sort of inverted 'V', will also help channel the horse straight (as already used in the early stages of training), and particularly one that tends to 'screw' over his fences. Be careful not to make the V too tight – by putting the poles on the fence too close together – to start with; the horse will

STRIDE DISTANCE CHART

An approximate guide to the distance/stride length, assuming that a horse's stride is 3m or thereabouts.
Read the chart vertically and then horizontally to ascertain the distance
e.g. a parallel to a vertical (two non-jumping strides) = 11.0m

APPROACH FROM:	To a VERTICAL (1 non-jumping stride)	VERTICAL (2 non-jumping strides)	PARALLEL (1 non-jumping stride)	PARALLEL (2 non-jumping strides)	SPREAD (1 non-jumping stride)	SPREAD (2 non-jumping strides)
VERTICAL	8.0m	11.0m	7.60m	10.80m	7.50m	10.80m
PARALLEL	7.85m	11.0m	7.30m	10.80m	7.50m	10.65m
SPREAD	8.10m	11.30m	7.85m	11.0m	–	–

*These distances may alter slightly depending on the horse's length of stride

training

be wary of the jump's strange appearance and you don't want him to back off too much and risk a refusal.

If the horse drifts, say to the left, use an open right rein as you approach the fence to encourage him to keep straight. If he persists in drifting, place a pole on the left side of the schooling fence, one end resting on the front rail and then the other end on the ground; also, a pole placed on the ground at right-angles to, and on the left side of the fence, may help to correct him. For horses that drift right, reverse the positions of the poles.

A pole placed diagonally across a fence (the high end of the pole near the top of the upright) also helps to stop a horse drifting; this can also be effective for a horse that persists in dropping a knee – for example, if he doesn't tuck up his left forearm as he jumps, place a pole with the *left* end high on the upright; if he drops a right knee, put the right end high.

All these corrective exercises can be used on single fences, or incorporated into a grid.

 Two poles placed to make an inverted 'V' which helps to channel the horse so that he jumps straight

I would obviously not ask as much of a novice as I would a Grade A because this sort of work is mentally as well as physically demanding; so for the novice we would keep the distances 'true', or nearly so, and not 'alter' them as we would for a more experi-enced horse ('true' and 'altered' distances are discussed in the next section). And again, the key to success is to keep the horse ticking over without overfacing him on making him stale; always keep that little bit extra for the ring. I play it by ear: why go on jumping and jumping at home if a horse is going well in the arena? If corrective schooling is needed, or the horse needs sharpening up a little bit, then we deal with the situation when it happens. There is no rule that cannot be broken when training horses, and something which works well for one will not necessarily work for another. And to try and rush things is *always* a mistake!

This sequence illustrates how poles can be used to form a channel which literally guides the horse towards the centre of the jump. This type of fence formation is particularly good if you have a horse that has a tendency to run out or drift to one side of a jump. The rider should always be aware of which direction this is likely to happen and use the appropriate hand and leg contact to guide the horse in a straight line.

Look how well the horse is approaching this fence. We take off on a good stride; it is a small, inviting fence, and an ideal confidence booster for a novice horse. The channel has guided him to the centre of the jump and he realises that there is no alternative but to go straight through and over the fence. He is really quite enjoying this!

The horse really stretches over the fence and lands perfectly in readiness for the next jump

All our schooling from this stage on is largely designed to teach a horse how to cope with the different distances he will meet in combinations, and with fences set at a related distance. All showjumping courses are based on a stride length of 12ft(3.6m); more critically, combinations and related distaces in show-jumping are also built around this 12ft(3.6m) stride – the fences for a simple one-stride double will therefore in theory be 24ft(7.2m) apart: 6ft(1.8m) for landing, 6ft for take-off and 12ft(3.6m) for the stride in-between. This is a 'true' distance: for 2 strides between the fences it would be 36ft(11m); for 3 strides 48ft(15m); and so on. Your horse's natural length of stride is unlikely to match this average exactly and will almost certainly be slightly longer or slightly shorter. Boysie was a very long-striding horse whereas Clover has a short, bouncy stride; the rider has to adjust his technique accordingly. To find out how it differs, set up two vertical fences 24ft(7.2m) apart – the 'true' distance for one theoretically easy, non-jumping stride: if he comes up really close to the second element his stride in the middle is too long, and you thereby discover that it is longer than the average; if he lands and in one stride is too far off to jump the second element nicely – or at all – it is too short (for the average). This experiment will help you determine the *pace* at which you must work your horse so he is as near as possible to a 12ft(3.6m) stride: for example if he has a very short stride you will have to push his jumping canter into quite a fast rhythm to make him open up until he is covering the ground with the desired 12ft-length stride; if he fails to achieve this, he will always tend to come too short in 1- and 2-stride combinations. Conversely a very long-striding horse must learn to be shorter and rounder in his way of going if he is to cope successfully with combinations.

If the horse has been going well through grids, his introduction to doubles and trebles should pose very few problems, particularly if to start with the distances between the jumps are made to suit his natural stride – he will arrive at exactly the right place to make a perfect jump out over the second and third elements. Again, height is not too important. How successfully the horse jumps through any combination depends very much on his rider's judgement as he approaches the first element: firstly in his judgement of pace, and then his accuracy in presenting the horse at the best point for take-off.

Technically the ideal take-off position for a fence is one and a third times its height away from its base; and the horse can take off either side of this point within a zone measuring a quarter of the height of the jump, and still clear it safely. For example, if the fence is 4ft(1.22m) high, the ideal take-off would be 5ft 3in(1.6m) each side of it. This is in an ideal world! In fact the bigger the fence, the less the margin of error, and particularly with oxers when the horse will have to come in close and really use himself in proper bascule to make a good, clean jump.

Judgement of stride is difficult even for the best of us, and it would be remarkable if we arrived at exactly the right spot every time. Various things that affect length of stride must therefore be borne in mind. For example, if you jump the first fence of a combination off a rather long stride, the distance between the first and second fence will be made shorter – in this case you must sit up and 'hold' with a steady hand (*not* a pulling one or the horse's head will come up too sharply and he will hollow) for a short stride (or strides). And if you come in rather too slow and short to the first fence the horse will land short and the distance to the next fence will be that much longer – if you have only one stride you will have to sit down and ride him strongly after landing to meet the second fence at the correct place for take-off. Obviously, the more strides you have between fences, the more scope you have for adjustment – so if you land short and have three strides, all you will need to do is ask the horse to lengthen a bit and you will arrive 'right' for the second fence. And again, how you react will depend on whether you are riding a long- or a short-striding horse.

Length of stride is also affected by the state of the going, and how the fences are sited; this is one of the most important things to assess when you walk a showjumping course before a competition – you should *always* ask yourself 'How will these conditions affect the way a horse goes, and *my* horse in particular?' In deep or heavy going or when the fences are sited – even slightly – uphill, the stride will be shorter; good going and downhill it will be longer. In a restricted area – an indoor school, a small ring – it will be shorter, as it will on hard summer ground.

So, all these different factors will affect the way a horse goes, and we must get to know our young horse thoroughly and train him accordingly so as a partnership we can cope with the problems we may meet when tackling a course of jumps, and in particular a combination. If we do make a bad approach and jump the first element too short or too long, the horse will have to be exceptionally clever to clear the second part and many less experienced horses will simply duck out to one side. I would try to avoid anything like this from happening from the very outset, because once the horse knows it can run out at the second part this tendency can be quite difficult to put right. I always do all I can to make the horse concentrate on where he is going, and do my best to bring him in at the right pace. Many riders seem to develop a fear of combinations, and in reaction tend to rush the horse too much, instead of letting the fence come to him and finding the right stride with the horse's rhythm.

Pages 93–7: Introduction to combinations
1: Patricia is schooling the mare over a simple grid which is the first stage of introducing the youngster to combinations. The grid comprises a cross pole, a canter pole, a small upright, one stride then out over a small parallel – it is termed 'gymnastic' jumping

2: The mare lands well over the small cross jump and it is worth noting how calmly she has entered the grid. Starting with a cross fence means that the horse has to approach the grid on a central line and this in turn will encourage the youngster to take the same line through the following elements. Combinations cause the majority of run outs in the arena, and if the approach is not correct it is all too easy for the horse to make a swift side exit; it is best if the horse never realises that this is a possibility

4: The mare continues on her central line and takes off for the second fence. She has popped over the canter pole and springs immediately over the upright. The pole on the ground has forced her to really use her hocks so that she can 'snap up' her front legs with relative ease

t r a i n i n g

3: On landing, the canter pole encourages the mare to take a slight check, taking one even stride in preparation for the second jump. On no account should the rider rush the horse. Patricia sits quietly but firmly, not interfering with the mare and by doing this encouraging her to find her own stride

5: Here she is mid-air and concentrating well on what she is doing. She looks keen to tackle the final element, the parallel. Patricia sits well and the mare makes it all look quite easy

The speed of the approach will depend upon the nature of the jumps in the combination. Here are two examples.

1 An upright, one stride to an upright, one stride to a parallel.

This sort of combination needs a relatively steady approach, the rider should keep the horse 'up in hand' as he jumps the upright elements. This allows the horse to bascule more over each jump and creates more space between the fences so there is a nice even stride out to the parallel. The approach should be more collected so the horse can then expand rather like a spring, over the last part of the combination which not only requires height, but also width.

2 A parallel, one stride to a parallel, one stride to an upright.

The rider needs to ride into this sort of combination with a little more pace in order to clear the width of the parallels. If the horse jumps the first part well, the rider should be careful not to 'chase him' and should sit relatively still so as not to interfere with him – in which case he will have a better chance of jumping the second part smoothly. On landing over the second parallel, the horse should then be in just about the right position to take one comfortable stride to jump out. This is quite a good combination for a young horse, and should help to build up his confidence.

6: This photograph is a very good example of how a horse assesses the height and width over a jump, and the importance of having clear groundlines.

Having landed from the upright, Patricia uses her legs to ask the mare to stretch and achieve enough impulsion to clear the parallel – she is really going for it

7: Taking off over the final element: a truly perfect jump for a young horse. I never build grids higher than 3ft 9in(1.1m) even for my advanced horses, and constantly change their layout to add more variety to the schooling

Overcoming problems through combinations

If the horse is struggling through a combination it may be that the distances are just too difficult for his natural length of stride and stage of training. Don't confuse him by asking the impossible, because he will only end up knocking the jumps down or running out. Run-outs are remarkably common at combinations, either through rider-error or simply because the horse doesn't have the confidence to tackle fences which come at him in such quick succession. Given time, he will get used to them; and if the rider continues to be quietly determined, but at the same time careful not to interfere with the horse's rhythm or to 'chase' him which can throw him off balance, he should eventually overcome his lack of confidence. In fact I am very firm with any horse that tries to run out, and if he persists in trying to duck out say, to the left, I will always carry my whip on that side. Don't be afraid of using it, either: the rider must be firm from the outset and indicate to the horse he has *every* intention of jumping *every* jump. Whether the horse is a novice or Grade A, it will soon sense if the rider is approaching in a half-hearted fashion, and will be very quick to take advantage of the situation.

A rider who sits too loosely in the saddle will not be able to use seat and legs effectively to guide the horse through a combination, with the result that the horse drifts out to the side. I see *so* many riders make this sort of mistake – it is rather like driving a car without a steering wheel or accelerator. Another common fault is not jumping the centre of the fences, making it even easier for the horse to run out. Moderate and bad riders do not bother to check their riding position and correct these mistakes; a good rider, however, will try his very best to sort out each problem as it arises, and put right his mistakes whenever he possibly can.

If the horse is not concentrating and looking where it is going it will inevitably run into difficulties – anybody watching this sort of partnership will soon appreciate the startling lack of trust and co-ordination between horse and rider, and it will be quite obvious that they will be most unlikely to negotiate a combination successfully. These two will really have run out before they even get there!

A horse may end up knocking elements down if he has been overfaced, and in this case everything must be done to help him regain his confidence: reduce the height and width of the fences, make grids simple, make jumping *fun*. However, if the rider knows that normally the horse will jump an upright to a parallel every time, or a good double without problems, then his carelessness is out of character and you should ask *why?*: has he been over-jumped? Is he maybe stale? Gone 'over the top'? Strained a muscle? Has the going got too hard for him? Is he just being lazy? A horse that really *is* being lazy is more than likely to knock fences down anywhere on the course and not just through combinations, and will never be careful enough to become a successful showjumper.

Training for related distances

An indication of how successfully the horse has been schooled on the flat lies in his willingness and ability to lengthen and shorten his stride correctly; this shows that the rider has control of his back end and can regulate his impulsion and energy either to accelerate or reduce pace exactly when he wants to. To achieve this sort of control is the main reason I spend so much time training my horses to be obedient to my aids, and is the key to jumping clear rounds. For example, a good rider will be able to dictate the number of strides the horse takes between two jumps set at a related distance. A useful exercise to practise this is to set up two uprights 60ft(18m) apart: this is a 'true' distance for

t
r
a
i
n
i
n
g

four non-jumping strides, so you set your horse cantering at his 12ft-length canter stride and approach in that rhythm – he should jump the first fence and then have four even strides before taking off for the second upright. If the pace is wrong for the length of stride this is rider error and the striding will be wrong for the distance – the horse will end up on a half-stride, perhaps, either too close to, or too far from the second upright.

Once you have trained yourself to judge the pace for a level four strides between these two fences, you can vary the exercise by taking five strides – come in more slowly, keep the hand steady and 'hold' the horse so he takes five level strides. These two fences can be set any number of strides apart – four, five or six – and to teach yourself and the horse to adjust his length of stride you can add or take away a stride within that distance, so that he lengthens and shortens on demand. A course designer may well reduceb or lengthen 'true' distances between fences slightly, to test the rider's skill and the horse's obedience in doing this. There are countless exercises using 'altered' distances to practise this lengthening and shortening of stride between fences. A basic canter grid with 'altered' distances could be set up as follows:

and will probably flatten the fence. It is a great feeling when the young horse at last begins to understand what you want him to do, and responds to your aids with smooth, willing alacrity as if you were pushing buttons to operate him. On the other hand, if the horse is not going well on the flat and is constantly evading his rider, it would be surprising if he ever jumped a clear round because he will not be listening to the alterations being asked of him as he comes to each fence. And far too many riders just muddle their way round courses, then wonder why their horses refuse and knock fences down all the time, ending up with a positive cricket score of faults. However, if riders are conscientious and follow a basic schooling programme, then everything is much more likely to come right in the arena.

I find canter poles particularly useful for regulating a horse's length of stride; they have even helped with some of my best horses which had problems keeping an even stride. Silver Dust was very bad at doing this, and found jumping indoors particularly difficult because fences came on him so quickly. By using canter poles, I usually manage to achieve consistency in the length of stride – though it often takes time and patience to build up a horse's confidence. And a brave,

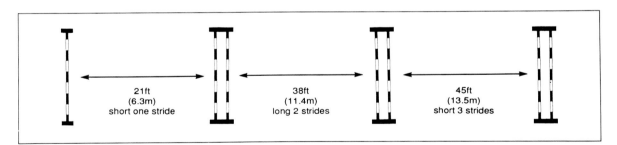

The horse must be listening to the rider and move along between the 2nd and 3rd fence to manage the longer 2 strides; and after the 3rd fence he must be ready to listen and shorten up so as not to bury himself under the 4th fence. The number of strides and the distances can be altered to make all sorts of variations. Whatever you do, never rush! This will only encourage the horse to lunge forwards, he will not be listening to the rider

intelligent horse will usually jump most fences once he has complete confidence in his rider and in what he is being asked to do. However, there is never any disgrace attached to horse and rider going back to basics and practising over smaller jumps. If the horse has lost confidence, then constantly overfacing him is not only highly foolish on the rider's part, but can ruin a potentially decent showjumper for life.

3   2

1: A steady approach to the first element ensures that the horse will not jump too flat, and prevents him from landing on the pole on the ground. By approaching a combination from the correct angle and at the right speed, the chances of popping over all the elements are much greater. If the entry is wrong it is difficult to correct the situation between jumps. Remember the golden rule – sit quietly and let the jumps come to you

t
r
a
i
n
i
n
g

5   4

4: This lapse in concentration has led to the horse rolling the pole with his back leg, and down it comes. By using my voice, I quietly ask him to settle on his approach to the final element. Vocal encouragement is important, particularly where youngsters are concerned, but this does not mean 'yelling' your way around the arena!

2&3: In these photographs the canter pole takes him slightly by surprise, and his concentration lapses for a moment. This is fairly typical of many youngsters, and I had to sit deep in the saddle and guide the horse through using contact between my leg and hand – kicking and flapping serves no purpose but to fluster the horse

5: From this we can see that the pole has fallen but the youngster is really firing on all cylinders for the final parallel and clears it with ease. It is important to construct a variety of different grids to accustom the horse to as many different layouts as possible, but I must stress that striding should be exact at all times

Rushing

Horses that rush fences are almost bound to knock poles down, particularly if the obstacle is an upright fence, because they are jumping flat. If they approach too fast their stride is almost certainly too long and so less easy to correct, and if they jump off a long stride they cannot bascule properly because they are too long and hollow in the back. However, with patience and correct training this is a habit which can sometimes be overcome.

If I have a young horse that rushes its fences, I will place those invaluable canter poles in front of the jump; by using about four poles the horse is encouraged to steady up

Canter poles placed at set intervals on the approach to the jump are particularly useful for a horse that rushes its fences

and regulate his stride. It may be that the rider does not have sufficient control, or does not really know how to steady a horse properly on the approach to a jump. For a novice or less experienced rider, nothing more severe than a vulcanite pelham and a correctly fitted martingale should be used to stop their horses. A pelham will help to control a keen horse, but is not so sharp that it will damage his mouth and hurt him as he jumps should the rider get 'left behind' thus knocking his confidence. Besides, too severe a mouthpiece will very often have an opposite effect and *make* a horse fuss about and pull, particularly if the rider is heavy-handed – as soon as the rider 'asks' him to steady, he will snatch and poke his head and rush off in nervous reaction. Rushing is so often caused

by the rider who is over-anxious when coming in to a fence, who tends to bottle the horse up and then fires him at it; instead he should hold the horse together on the approach to the jump, keeping that nice steady rhythm and making the horse use its hocks to spring over the fence. If you sit still and let the fence come to the horse, he is less likely to rush. It may take some time to settle a strong, excitable horse and there will always be some that have some strange 'quirk' in the arena and resort to rushing.

Similarly, if a horse tears off after a fence he will never be balanced enough to manage, say, a related stride to an upright and jump it cleanly. To a certain extent this can be corrected – the important thing is *not* to grab at him and haul him up the minute he lands from a fence; this will almost certainly worry him and in anticipation he may start jumping with his head in the air (and therefore hollow), or will rush even more, or may even be persuaded to refuse. Rather, let him land and take a few strides, then sit up and quietly steady him – circle if necessary, not too tight, until he comes back to trot.

Running out

I find the most effective way of dealing with a horse that persistently runs out is to place those two guiding poles – the inverted 'V' – on each side of a jump, as we sometimes do in the early training sessions (see page 61). The horse can clearly see the channel that is formed, and will be more easily persuaded that there is no alternative but to go straight through and over the middle of the jump. Running out is often the fault of the rider, as we have said before: if a rider fails to keep his horse between hand and leg as he approaches a fence he will find it very difficult to keep him straight. When you correct a horse that runs out, *always* turn him back *towards* the fence – so if he goes out to the left, turn him back to the right; if he ducks to the right, use the left rein to turn him. Once you are re-organised, present him at the fence again, straight, and carry a whip on the side the horse is inclined to rush off to. Don't approach too fast, as the faster you go the harder it is

to hold him together and keep him straight – and if he tries it again, don't be scared to give him a firm smack down the shoulder with the whip. Sometimes it is better to approach in trot, if you keep the fences low, because it is easier to keep control.

As with any obedience problem, the rider must be careful to establish the cause of the trouble – whether the horse really is being naughty or whether he has lost confidence and is fearful. Have you asked him correctly, and has he understood what is wanted? Have you asked too much of him? Has the going got too hard/deep for him, making jumping a trial, rather than a pleasure, for him? If it is fear, then the horse needs to be taken over smaller fences to regain his trust and enthusiasm. Sometimes a break for a day or two – even a week – will restore zest and courage.

Refusing

Refusing and running out are the same sort of disobedience. Usually the 'stopper' will be putting on the brakes a few strides away from the fence, and the rider must immediately use legs and voice to encourage the horse to attempt the jump as soon as he senses this happening. Horses sometimes learn to stop simply because the rider doesn't keep enough leg 'on' in the approach to a jump. If the horse has been overfaced he may react by stopping, so again, lower the fences slightly to regain his confidence. A young horse can perhaps be forgiven for stopping once if he is really green and spooky, but if we have been abiding by our training programme and our policy of never asking him to attempt anything before he is ready, then the ball is in his court: he must learn at the outset to go forward, and if he stops again he will get a good telling off so he understands clearly that stopping is wrong and not popular, and will not be tempted to repeat his mistake. Dismantle the fence to poles on the ground if he persists in stopping, because if you let him stop again and again it will become a habit: within the first two or three attempts he must be taught that he *goes forward* through those wings, and nowhere else! Sadly, some horses are born stoppers and will never jump successfully.

Practice courses

The best way to introduce a horse to all sorts of obstacles is to construct simple courses at home. I will often use plastic bags, coloured string, even pots of flowers from the garden to make fences more spooky so as to accustom my young horses to the bright colours they will see all around them, and especially in the arena when they go to a show. It is extremely annoying when you know a horse is quite capable of jumping a course but won't concentrate because he is so busy spooking at everything else round about. We make all sorts of fences and obstacles at Quendon, including water, ditches and even a Derby bank!

Constructing a variety of jumps is an essential part of our 'homework' in preparation for the real thing

A water obstacle can take the young horse a little while to get used to, and should not be too wide and intimidating to start with. There are no water fences in novice competitions, but it is an extremely good idea to introduce the horse to this sort of obstacle as early as possible. With a plain water jump it is wise to put a rail over the water to start with, or place a small brush fence either in front of it or as 'wings' to help the horse measure the width of it and encourage him to make a clean and positive jump over – and not through! – it. Water always requires positive riding because a young horse tends to look down at the last minute and will sometimes 'cat leap' the obstacle. Never use corrugated iron as a substitute for water because it can

*t
r
a
i
n
i
n
g*

We can see how the horse is stretching to clear this ditch – he is really using himself. This type of jump can be easily constructed if you have a field and adds variety to the standard showjumping fences. We have even built a Derby Bank at Quendon

cause such ghastly injury. Some people place blue fertiliser bags in trays on the floor to give the appearance of water – but there is really nothing like the real thing for practise.

Water jumps should be approached like spreads, with speed and impulsion. In advanced competitions, a course builder will often test the rider's control and the horse's obedience by building an upright after a water jump, usually on a related stride; if the rider is unable to collect the horse again as soon as he lands from the water, he will not succeed in getting the height over the upright.

A young horse should also be introduced to water trays at quite an early stage. Place two trays under a low cross-pole but well apart so there is a gap in the middle: for his first attempt the horse will jump just the pole – if the trays fill him with terror so he won't go near them at all, take the pole away altogether so all he has to do is walk between them. As his confidence grows, build the jump up gradually: replace the cross-pole, and pull

Style becomes before height. This is only a small cross pole with a canter pole on the approach run but schooling over such jumps constantly helps the novice to improve its technique

the water trays in a little bit at a time until eventually there is no gap and he is jumping pole and trays, like an old 'un!

Courses are becoming increasingly varied and technical and nowadays often incorporate ditches, banks and water. Furthermore course builders are seeking to test not just how high and wide the horse can jump, but also his agility and obedience, and will often set 'altered' distances through doubles and trebles and between single fences that demand maximum control and ability to adapt length of stride. Certainly this is true in more advanced competition; at novice level course builders are kinder, and will not make courses too 'technical' – the aim here is to encourage the young horse to jump confidently and cleanly.

This does not mean that a novice competition doesn't present an adequate test of obedience and 'manoeuvrability'. With this in mind I build courses at home that require the horse to turn in all directions, and I never keep jumping the same course time after time otherwise he will risk becoming blasé and careless. The jumps should never be so big as to overface the horse and shake his confidence, but they must nevertheless be high

enough to test his ability and courage; jumping very small jumps all the time can cause problems because the horse will not be learning to use himself properly and it will come as a shock when he is asked to jump larger fences. A good trainer will strike just the right balance between asking the horse for a little bit more so as to keep him keen and on his toes, but not so much as to knock his confidence and his trust in his rider. I make sure there is a good variety of fences, and will incorporate a combination or two somewhere in the course.

The whole point of jumping practice courses is to help the horse establish a regular showjumping rhythm, and to build up his trust and confidence in the rider and his willingness to be obedient to the rider's aids. To this end, when schooling I will always insist on the young horse balancing himself properly in the corners of an arena and on turns, rather than cutting in; only in this way will he be able to assess and measure a fence properly before he jumps it. And as always: if the approach is not correct, the horse will never be able to jump to the best of his ability. When you are practising at home, if

you are really completely wrong as you come in to a jump, circle round and try for a better approach — after all, that is why we practise. However, don't do this so often that it becomes a habit before every fence, or you will be teaching the horse to refuse: forward and straight is the first and foremost requirement, a really forward-thinking, positive attitude from horse *and* rider!

It is always a temptation to over-jump a horse, and I never feel it is necessary to jump my horses every single day – so often this results in a horse getting careless, or fed up and stale. I like to finish on a good note, and leave a bit of sparkle for another day – and always leave at least 25 per cent of the horse's jumping effort for the competition. I only really jump my Grade As if there is a problem, as they do enough in the arena. However, I would jump the novices about three times a week using different grids and simple courses. The whole point of a methodical training programme is that although you are always building on the horse's education and asking for a little more every day, you should never ask him to do something that will destroy his faith in you.

3 COMPETING

Whether you are competing at the top of the show-jumping ladder or just occasionally for fun, you should still experience the same 'buzz' when you enter the arena. Even though I compete four or sometimes five days a week, I still get enjoyment out of showjumping and there is a great sense of achievement to be experienced when everything goes right on the big day.

Where young horses are concerned, competing can be even more satisfying as you begin to see all your hard work at home pay off in the arena – all those fraught moments when you have considered giving it all up as a bad job are suddenly forgotten! It is easy to get too ambitious if a young horse starts its compettitve career well, and I have seen far too many horses overjumped by the time they are six-year-olds and ruined for life; striking the right balance and making steady progress is more important than aiming for a red rosette each time you go into the arena. Unfortunately, we sometimes learn this lesson through our own mistakes when it is too late to rectify the situation. Once a horse starts to refuse in the arena and gets totally bored with the job it is a time-consuming problem to correct – sometimes you never can, and a potentially good horse can be ruined.

There is always the temptation to overjump a horse if you are going through a particularly successful phase, but this is the time to take a grip on yourself and think how this might affect the situation in time to come. You can never be sure what is going to happen with horses, and this is propbably part of their great attraction!

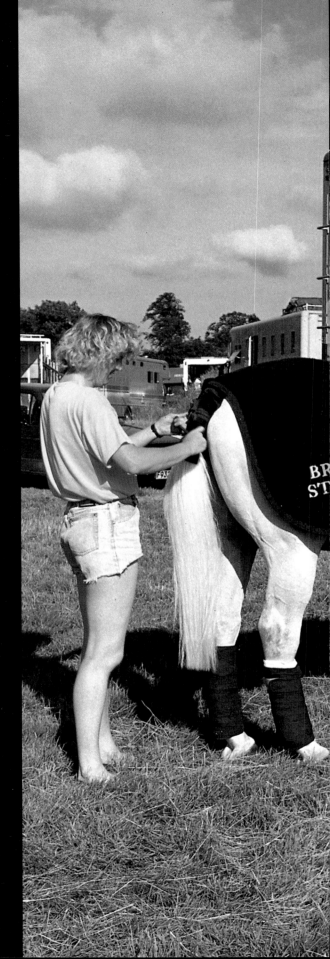

Early Competition

At last ...we make it to the show. Gill prepares Silver
Dust for our first class

TEAM
BROOK STREE
HORSES
ROBERT SMITH
INTERNATIONAL COMPETITION HORSES
BOUGHT AND SOLD
CONTACT
ROBERT SMITH
TEL:(0799)
HIGHBARN
B852 HRM

There is no better experience for the young horse than for him to take part in the real thing. I like to jump my novices at as many shows as possible so they become accustomed to all the strange sights and sounds, the exciting atmosphere, and to many different courses. By the time our training programme has got to the two weeks or so leading up to a show, ideally the horse will have reached the stage where he is ticking over nicely – any particular problems will have been sorted out, and he will be happy and settled in all his basic schooling work. I would therefore do no more than jump him over some simple courses at home once or maybe twice in these weeks. At his first competition I would be aiming for him to get a nice clear round, and would certainly not push him too much at this stage as regards speed or clever turns. Some horses that are jumping very well at home find all the activity at a showground altogether too exciting and distracting to concentrate properly on what they are supposed to be doing, and most youngsters on their first outing will invariably regress as regards composure and co-operative behaviour.

Many people will take their young horse to a show just to 'have a look round'; personally I always think it is more valuable for the horse's experience to go into the arena and actually attempt a proper course – though *never* at the risk of overfacing him. Really, I don't have time to take horses to shows if they are not going to reap full benefit from the trip by competing, however low the status of the class. For this, clear round jumping is an excellent way to introduce a horse to jumping away from home; usually you are allowed to continue round a clear round course until you have completed it, however many times the horse stops – unlike a 'proper' competition where if you have three refusals it means elimination and no chance of working through a problem if the horse stops or spooks at any one particular jump. You can also have as many 'go's' as you like; though two should be enough, even if the first one proved sticky! This sort of competition can only build confidence. Equally helpful are the many shows where the organisers will allow riders to school their horses over the jumps in the arena at the end of the day when the competition has finished. It is well worth taking advantage of this opportunity should it arise and I may take my young horses round the course several times. Some horses do find jumping in new surroundings most strange, and a 'schooling outing' such as this is an excellent way to build up their confidence.

There are many classes at both unaffiliated and affiliated shows (registered to the BSJA) which are suitable for novice horses. Although it may seem intimidating to take the young horse straight into affiliated competitions, some of the classes for novices such as Discovery and Newcomers' competitions (see p134) are really quite small; so, having successfully tackled clear rounds, I would normally enter my novices in one of these 'beginner' competitions. And once you have decided which your first show will be, your final preparations for the novice horse's first proper outing can begin.

 ## The week before

I like to keep my novice fresh and 'on the boil' for his show. If the competition is at the weekend, I would probably let him have the Monday off as a day's rest. On the Tuesday and Wednesday I would school him lightly and maybe take him out for a hack for 3/4 hour. An occasional brisk canter will clear the wind (but make sure the ground is good).

Thursday would be the day I would work him over a practice course to make sure he was still jumping well and on course for the forthcoming competition; and if I was not happy with the way he was going, he would be schooled and jumped again the following day to try and iron out any problems with his jumping. If the young horse had gone well on

the Thursday, I might just walk him out on the Friday or school him lightly.

By this time my novices will have reached quite a high level of fitness; according to their temperament, they may well be receiving slightly more energy-giving feed, though not the highly-strung ones who are bound to be even more excitable at their first show. If I feel that a horse is getting lazy I would hack it out in an attempt to 'sweeten' it and stimulate some enthusiasm. An experienced horseman will know the difference between a sluggish horse and a horse that is off-colour. It may be that its feed can be changed slightly to increase its energy – sluggishness very

Training at home before a show is essential but we always resist the temptation to jump our horses too much. I prefer to save that little extra for the competition

often results from boredom so try to vary the work pattern as much as possible. The odd pipe-opener in stimulating countryside will do any horse a power of good, and give him that extra bit of sparkle. My horses always seem to be altogether more spirited anyway when hacking, Silver Dust particularly; even though he is a mature horse there are some things he just never seems to get used to! When I lived in Yorkshire with my father we used to hack out over the moors, and this sort of exercise was a wonderful tonic for them. As always, it all goes back to the importance of knowing the individual horse and establishing the right balance between feed and performance – what sort of food and how much dictating to a certain extent the way a horse will behave.

We always practise loading a young horse into the horsebox well before show day, as there is nothing more infuriating if he refuses to go in $1/4$ hour before you are due to leave. Everyone becomes tense and irritated and even if the horse does decide eventually to go in, he will probably be too upset to concentrate and do his best when finally he gets into the ring. It can be a very bad start to the day! So a few days before the show, practise loading. It is a good idea to dress him up, not in full travelling gear (for which see p115), but with bandages or special travelling boots to protect his legs, knee-boots in case he slips up, and maybe a poll guard if he is in the habit of chucking his head up – competition horses are valuable, and an injury sustained in the course of this sort of exercise would be too silly. You have more control if the horse has his bridle on, but use a snaffle and lead him with a halter rope – or better still a lunge line – attached to the off-side bit-ring and threaded through the near-side (having taken the reins off altogether). We park the horsebox or trailer next to a wall or in a gateway to discourage the horse from diving off the edge of the ramp if there are no ramp-gates, and with a lunge rein attached to one side of the lorry and brought round behind him, encourage him to walk up the ramp – if he is stubborn the lunge can be brought up round his quarters (helpers are essential for this operation). Occasionally you come across an imaginative and way-wise character who decides he can easily evade the issue by standing on end and swinging round so his front legs land either on top of, or on the other side of the lunge. Then you will need two helpers to try 'handing him in' – a helper each side with hands crossed behind his quarters, just as a recalcitrant racehorse is handed into a starting stall. It is almost as important to have a 'schoolmaster', too, an older horse who will walk calmly up and down the ramp just to 'show the way', and will lead into the lorry first and stand quietly munching hay. One or other of these methods usually works well with an apprehensive loader; lead him in and out two or three times, and he will soon be accustomed to trailer or horsebox.

We like to have all the tack clean and ready the day before the competition, and we always take spare stirrup leathers, reins, girths and other odd items of tack in the event of something breaking at the last minute. We also prefer to take our own first-aid kits and grooming equipment. If the horse is staying overnight at the show – the usual routine if the competition is a fair distance away – there is even more preparation to be done. However, an overnight stay will definitely help a horse to settle before a competition, since he will have had a better chance of recovering from the journey. Gill always checks the vaccination certificates in good time before a show to make sure that we have them all – one per horse! – and that they are up to date; this should save one last-minute panic. We always take our own hay and feed, and stick as closely to our daily routine as we can; changing the feed at the last minute can be particularly upsetting for a horse, so ours will always receive exactly the same as usual – although 'breakfast' will have to be cut down if a horse's class comes up early in the morning. We take our own bedding materials too, because very often you arrive at the stable and find that a different sort of bedding has been used; many horses will eat a straw bed – particularly if they are affected by the dust and you don't want them to! – and the last thing you need to see the night before a competition is your winner-to-be stuffing himself with straw!

Always make sure you have packed the appropriate clothes for the competition, too: a hacking jacket is the accepted dress for novice competitions, and a show jacket for Grade B upwards.

The more you compete, the more easily you will move into your 'travelling routine' – and ultimately will never forget to pack that crucial item of tack!

Travelling to the show

All our horses are fully protected when they are travelling in the horsebox. We bandage all four legs very carefully, either with wool-mix travelling bandages with plenty of gamgee-type padding underneath, or padded velcro-fastened travel boots; these are very popular nowadays, although in times of real crisis, which is just when you want them to do their job properly, they have been known to slip or even come undone. Horses tend to get rather hot when they are travelling and a novice unaccustomed to being in the horsebox is quite likely to break out into a sweat. For this reason we always travel our horses with an anti-sweat rug under a lightweight day rug, even during the summer, to prevent them catching a chill. Some people use a poll guard, particularly if a horse tends to throw his head about anyway and risks banging his head on the roof; many horses have been made nervous of travelling because they have knocked themselves in this way, and they never seem to connect the blow with their own fidgety behaviour. Tails always seem to rub in a lorry, so ours are bandaged and protected with a tail guard which fastens to the rug. As

we have said, competition horses are worth a great deal of money; they may well be owned by a sponsor – or in part, at least – and so it is essential to wrap them up well to minimise the risk of injury while travelling.

A haynet will keep the horse occupied and help him to relax, and if the journey is very long he must be offered water at regular intervals to prevent dehydration. The horsebox should be light and well-ventilated to minimise over-heating and stress; similarly the footing must be good, as nothing will worry a horse more than if he feels insecure – there are many different types of anti-slip floor surfaces or matting on the market, and the latter also helps to relieve some of the pressure on legs as it has a 'cushioning' effect. And the less strain on the legs, the better the horse will perform (or should!).

With patience and practice the novice will soon be as sensible as the schoolmaster; I find that all my horses get used to travelling so quickly that we have very few problems.

Silver Dust is correctly dressed to travel in the horsebox. It really isn't worth taking unnecessary risks for the sake of taking a little extra time to bandage up properly

On arrival at the show

So you have completed your journey safely, have managed to find the showground without too many misdirections, and with influenza passports checked and approved by the inevitable official at the showground gates, have been allowed access to the show at last! If this is a day-trip and not an overnight stay, the first thing to do is to check the time of your classes so that you know exactly when to get each horse out of the horsebox to start warming up. If it is the young horse's first show, you will almost certainly have to unload him well before the competition to give him enough time to settle and take everything in. Tack him up and walk him round quietly, and he should gradually calm down and start to listen to his rider. For the real novice, find a quiet area just to walk him around, maybe working in circles, and try and persuade him to 'switch off' from all the other horses and start concentrating on what *you* want. And the long-accepted premise that a nervous and tense rider will transmit these negative vibes straight through to the horse is so true, and invariably leads to problems. Therefore it is vital that the rider is calm, confident but firm in his temper and with his aids; if he is, the horse is more likely to settle down.

I usually school my horses with draw reins when I am warming up for a competition. Having walked the horse round, I will trot in circles and figures of eights to try and keep his attention, and really to assess how well he is listening to me. On their first few outings many youngsters are quite likely to go round with their heads high in the air, and draw reins will help to reinforce the rider's aids.

Having a helper on the ground is essential with a young horse to help put jumps up, and just to give a helping hand when needed. When I am satisfied at walk and trot and feel that the horse is relaxing and co-operating, I will then ask him to pop over some small jumps. Sometimes the practice jump area can be hazardous with horses and riders flying in all directions, and it is then wise to go away for a bit and return when the area is quieter.

On arrival at the show, it is important to let the novice settle down quietly. I would start with a small fence, gradually increasing the height, but I would be careful not to ask too much. Some people go round and round a practice arena and end up with a sweaty, exhausted horse to take into the competition. You need to be able to judge exactly how long you warm up for a competition – it is a case of striking the right balance and knowing your horse well

competing

116

To start with I will usually ask for a small jump with a pole pushed out in front, and will simply trot over it to begin with; this will just steady the horse up and help him to concentrate. Go over the jump in both directions if you can, every now and then asking the horse to come back to halt and to rein-back a few steps; this will increase his engagement of the hocks and therefore achieve more collection. When he is performing well over a small jump, then we will try a higher upright followed by a spread. When warming up it is important not to exhaust the horse in order to calm it down: over-tired horses do not jump well, and working a young horse to a white lather does not augur well for jumping in the arena. On the other hand don't be so soft that he gets away with murder – I am a great believer in obedience from the start; but I never expect miracles the first time out, and in particular I like to think that the novice will relate the outing to a good experience.

Once the young horse has reached this stage in his training and has managed his first outing we hope with outstanding success, he should be ready to tackle the bigger affiliated courses: his career as a showjumper is now underway.

c o m p e t i n g

The first affiliated competition

This is the day we have all been working towards: our youngster's first 'proper' competition. To be eligible for British Show Jumping Association classes, both horse and rider must be affiliated to the association; basically this means registering your horse with details of the owner and usual rider, for a fee which is renewable every year (see p133). Even if our preparation included some clear round jumping this will not really compare with the sort of course we will meet in a BSJA affiliated jumping class, where the fences will be brighter and rather more grand-looking, of far greater variety, with heavier poles and much greater use of fillers than any we have schooled over in clear round classes and at home.

A show will always attract a reasonable number of spectators, and most novices will not have experienced crowd noise; inevitably a young horse will find this distracting on his first few outings, and at some of the larger shows there will be all sorts of strange things, particularly where rings are set out side by side. It will be just your luck that there are Pony Club mounted games or a carriage-driving competition just as you are going into the arena! But this is all part of the horse's education, and is one of the reasons why when we arrive at the show, we try to settle the young horse by walking him around and just letting him have a good look at everything.

This policy applies as much to the unaffiliated show as it does to the large affiliated one.

Some people spend months taking their youngsters to one unaffiliated competition after another to 'school' them. This is all very well, but the difference in standard between unaffiliated and affiliated competition is considerable when the size, appearance and colour of the fences, the weight of the poles and the technical problems demanded by the course as a whole are all taken into account. If the ultimate intention is to tackle affiliated competitions, surely it is better to try the horse in some of the BSJA classes as soon as possible, rather than wearing him out over smaller courses? There are affiliated classes which are designed specifically for young and novice horses, namely the Discovery, the Newcomers and the Pathfinder classes which provide an excellent introduction to competition work. All these courses are built by experienced course builders to particular specifications which include restrictions as to height and width of fences, to speed, and to technical difficulty, especially where distances are concerned. Some people feel intimidated of affiliated competition, and do not realise that the BSJA runs these special competitions for novices. However, there is nothing to stop anybody going along to watch some of these classes, to assess whether you are ready to enter this sort of competition.

Walking the course

Walking the course sounds easy, doesn't it? In fact it is the most crucial part of your preparation for jumping it: exactly how you will ride each fence and precisely what you will do in between needs to be thought out properly – and more importantly, these plans must be remembered once you are in the arena. Like many other riders I find that I concentrate much better if I walk the course by myself; this is not being anti-social but you *do* need to concentrate to walk a course properly, at any level of competition. First, we must obviously be careful to remember the order of the jumps – even some of the best riders have been known to have a sudden blank, but jumping the wrong course still means elimination, which is a sad end to any competition. Besides, lapses of memory do *not* lead to positive riding, and indecisive riding can be as disastrous on a Grade A horse as it almost certainly would be on a novice. Children on ponies can get away with precipitate changes of direction because ponies are incredibly agile and can turn on a sixpence, but horses are a different matter!

As you walk the course, consider in what way the course builder is seeking to test the competitors when he built it: the wide spread – or two spreads – followed by the upright gate to test obedience; the combination to test obedience and suppleness; the upright planks or box parallel off an awkward turn to test balance, pace and straightness – as much the rider's judgement; the narrow little stile placed towards the end of the course and often after large fences to test the rider's concentration – if he fails to set the horse up properly and give it due respect, down will come this relatively easy fence, placed for that very purpose. When I walk a course, I always go over it time after time in my head so that I know exactly what I am going to do, and where.

So we must remember direction; we must also pace out combinations and fences with related distances (usually about six horse-strides or less – the fewer there are the harder it is to ride, because there is less room to adjust the horse's stride). The rider should know how many of his paces are equivalent to the horse's length of stride. For novice tracks, course builders try to keep the striding easy and therefore comfortable for the horse, but as the competitions become more advanced, they will build bigger courses with more technical problems which require the rider to shorten and lengthen the stride of his horse for related distances; otherwise, if perfectly correct distances are always given, the jump-off – which is nearly always timed – develops into a race over big fences which is not good for any horse. Experienced course builders will therefore give problems of distance, and it is up to the rider to know exactly what these different distances are in relation to his horse, and to decide, as he walks the course, what his pace must be in his approach to a combination in order for his horse to fit in the desired number of strides. To re-cap, relative to the stride of 12ft(3.7m), a true 3-stride distance is 48ft(14.6m, or about 16 paces); 4 strides = 59ft(18m, or at 19 to 20 paces); 5 = 71ft(21.6m, or 23-24 paces); and 6 = 82ft(25m, about 27 paces). Altered distances can be set between individual fences so that, for example, the horse must shorten for five or lengthen for four strides to be 'right' for the 2nd fence; and in trebles (three fences with *one* non-jumping stride between) there may be two short distances which would have to be ridden steadily, or two long to be ridden strongly, or a true followed by a long or a short (in a *treble* you should not expect to meet a short followed by a long – or vice versa, which is worse – this would be bad course-building). A short distance is created by reducing the true distance by 1ft up to 18in(30–45cm), and a long one by increasing the true distance from 1 to 2ft(30-60cm); if these limits are exceeded they become too difficult for any horse and rider to manage – in the 1960 Olympic Games the treble had almost impossible distances and caused enormous trouble.

Other factors besides the experience of the horse will determine how you ride each fence: some horses are naturally longer striding than others, some are very short, so the distances presented in the course will need to be ridden accordingly; the sort of surface will affect how your horse goes, too – good old turf is best, but if it is deep or boggy, or baked hard in the sun your horse's stride will shorten. Always take careful note of the going over the whole line of the course: are there any boggy corners? Does the ground fall away anywhere, maybe at a place where I want to turn so it might unbalance the horse? In particular, what is it like in front of each jump, and what is the best line of approach? If I mis-judge the approach the horse may well refuse or knock a pole down. Bearing all this in mind, what studs would the horse be best to wear? And another point: if it is sunny, where will the sun be when I ride each fence? Will it cast shadows and perhaps make a false groundline? There are many points to take into consideration.

Walking the course correctly basically makes the difference between winning and losing in a competition. What looks a relatively simple exercise is actually quite a complex matter and it is not just a question of mapping out the direction in which you are required to go – that would be too easy!

Striding out distances between doubles and trebles, as well as related distances, is vital otherwise you are bound to run into problems, particularly with a novice; you need to help the horse around the course as much as possible. Make sure the distances are firmly implanted in your memory. Look out for certain landmarks round the outside of the arena which would serve as good indicators as to where to turn. Try to imagine how the horse will visualise each jump – is there a false groundline caused by shadows, and so on?

Finally, if you are unsure, walk the course again if there is time – better still, if possible, watch a few horses jump round the course and learn from their mistakes. There will be a plan of the course for the first round in the collecting ring, together with the jump-off course, which is useful to refresh your memory just before you are due to enter the arena

Riding the course

Every course will vary considerably, but the basic types of jump will stay the same and will include upright fences in the form of poles, planks, gates or walls, and spread fences such as the oxer and triple bar. Brightly coloured fences need a firm approach because young horses will tend to spook at them. I always wear spurs because they provide a gentle reminder to the horse to listen to my aids. Usually the first fence of any course will be quite inviting. When I go into the arena I always circle a few times on both legs and then bring the horse back onto his hocks by asking him to halt and rein back.

Although you shouldn't dally, there is no need to whizz through the start line as soon as the bell is rung. If the second fence is sited after a turn, approach the first fence in canter on whichever leg would be the correct lead for the turn; then your horse is balanced to attempt the second obstacle. Maybe the first fence is a vertical, in which case a fairly collected approach wil be needed, and from a left canter lead if there is a left turn to fence two. Let us say this is an inviting spread; having jumped the first in a collected way, I would ride into the corner of the arena looking at the second fence. As I turn I can increase my pace a little because I need to get well into the bottom rail of the spread so that my horse clears the width. We may then have a related distance of, say, about four strides to fence three: this is another vertical so I need a more collected approach, and must steady up immediately after the spread — a collected, shorter five strides would be better than a long four. After three, I may have to turn to the right, so I shift my weight to the right-hand side of the horse as he is jumping the vertical so that he lands with the off-fore leading (ie the correct lead for a right turn).

Fence four is a triple bar: I need to get the horse to lengthen its stride, but not so much that it stands off the jump and catches the back rail: the take-off needs to be as close as possible. The wall at fence five needs firm

riding as a young horse will probably spook, but I must not go so fast that the horse jumps flat, my legs maintain the impulsion, my hands keep a light but steady contact through the reins. I may need to use a half-halt having jumped the triple bar to get the horse back on its hocks ready for the wall at five.

Fence six is a double, the first part an oxer and the second an upright, with one true non-jumping stride between the two elements. The correct approach is crucial and I must use the corner of the arena properly so as to come in straight; and the horse should be going well into my hand to increase the impulsion and create that spring effect so essential to clear the first element, otherwise I am likely to have the front rail down. One easy stride, then straight over the second element. Fence seven is a rustic spread which should not pose too many problems, but I need now to be turning on the left rein for fence eight, the planks. Planks can fall down all too easily so accurate riding is needed here: I must hold the horse together with my legs and hands and almost lift him over the jump.

Fence nine is another oxer, and again I must wind the horse up like a spring and ride with enough impulsion. The filler is rather spooky, so this could be the 'bogey' fence. The treble at ten is all there is to tackle now, but this is quite demanding: a parallel, one true stride to a parallel, one long stride to an upright – then over the finish line. I would need more pace to clear the parallel elements, and I must ride over the centre of the jumps; it is so easy for a young horse to duck out at the side through combinations, particularly off a long stride, so it is vital to keep the leg on to guide him through. As long as the pace and impulsion of our approach are both right, there should be no problem with any of the three elements. It is crucial that the rider's concentration does not lapse.

Riding Silver Dust at Hickstead 1991 – he is one of my most consistent horses and, although not always a winner, is nearly always in the ribbons

c o m p e t i n g

122

This sequence of photographs shows how a horse judges and negotiates a jump. My weight is going with the horse's movement and has shifted slightly forward on the approach. We literally 'spring off' and stretch over the spread with relative ease. Watching riders and horses jump is the best way of learning horse/rider technique, and understanding this will help you to improve your jumping skills; we all learn from each other

Here is another sequence of shots showing horse and rider position on the approach to, and jumping, a spread. As the fences get wider and higher, correct speed and exact take-off are essential factors in clearing both the width and height of the jump

If you can, watch a few riders tackling the course before you are due into the arena, to see which fences are catching competitors out. However, as I have said already, no one should expect miracles from a young horse on his first few outings, and it is always up to his rider to help him as much as possible around the course. For example if he is on the wrong canter lead or disunited, or just needs steadying up when you are jumping, bring him back to trot and establish the correct lead for the next turn and the jump following it. It is all part of his education, and it could be the difference betwen a clear round and having faults. Besides, the rider must do everything he can to prevent the novice crashing through his fences; otherwise he might be put off jumping for ever.

The jump-off

How you ride a jump-off course depends entirely on the experience of the horse. I would never ask too much of the novice, and would just be aiming for a nice clear round; there may be places where I might ask for more speed, but at this stage I do think a rider should not be too ambitious – he must know the jump-off course intimately so that he can ride the shortest possible route without wasting a second, yet keep his demands on the horse within reasonable bounds. There may be places where even a young horse can turn tightly – but *not* at the expense of putting him off; it is infinitely preferable that the horse jumps a clear round rather than learns that he can flatten everything in sight! Always, the novice will need time to look at his fences and cannot be asked to turn on a sixpence; so the rider must be very careful in choosing his line. Inevitably a competitor will be at a disadvantage if he is drawn to go amongst the first in a jump-off, but if he has schooled and prepared the horse himself, he should know fairly well what it can do. Again, different fences will need a different approach: it is a big risk to gallop to a vertical because the horse is likely to jump flat; and turning too sharply into a fence may take a novice by surprise so that he refuses. I like to build up a good flowing pace, but without rushing or flustering the horse; though if you complete the course without mishap you can certainly gallop through the finish – every second counts and you have nothing to lose here.

Time faults
Remember that in BSJA competitions there is a time limit in the first round as well as in the jump-off; this means that the rider must maintain a reasonable pace throughout his round, and should select the shortest route wherever possible – without being rash – to avoid having time faults. Some time limits are very fair, others are extremely tight, and I like to watch the horses that go before me to see how easily they manage to achieve it – if they have time faults I will then watch to see where I can try and make up on the course; but I must admit that this is not an easy thing to judge when you are actually jumping the course. All things considered, on a young horse I would not be worrying too much about time, because my first priority would always be to go clear.

I am often asked how I judge the speed at which I am riding to ensure that I jump a round within the specified time. I think, by and large, the rider first has to establish whether his or her horse is a long- or short-striding horse to assess exactly how fast the horse is going. For example, a short-striding horse may seem to be going faster because his legs appear to be moving faster when in actual fact the longer striding of the two is covering the ground with greater speed. Showjumping is not like eventing when it is possible to glance at a stopwatch when going round the course – everything looms up far quicker in a showjumping arena and it is important that the rider does not lose

c o m p e t i n g

concentration. Having said that, very often there is a digital timer on display at one end of the arena, so it is sometimes possible to glance up at the time. I think a competitor gets a certain feel for speed and knows how far to push his or her horse, but this obviously comes with experience and practise. Obviously, the fewer strides you put in between fences the more economical you are going to be with your time. This is why it is so important to be able to lengthen and shorten your horse's strides.

Improving your technique

However brilliant your horse is, together you will never be very successful in the show-jumping arena if you can't ride it properly. You can never stop learning or improving your riding, and a great deal can be learnt by watching others, even by taking a video of yourself. My wife, Leanne, often videos me when I am jumping and I can then sit at home and see for myself how I might improve my own technique so as to help that particular horse; maybe my upper body leans slightly to one side of the horse's neck as he jumps (a common fault!) which increases his tendency to drift; perhaps my lower leg slips too far up the horse's side so when he lands I am not able to keep him straight. I find the video is an excellent means whereby I can really see how my position affects the horse's performance, and it undoubtedly helps me improve my riding technique. Moreover self-critical riders will always be willing to learn, and be open to new ideas, which can only be a good thing as there is *always* room for improvement in riding and horsemanship – this is its challenge! There is no better feeling than when you *know* you have jumped a really good round, and that you rode to the best of your ability when you were in the arena; and if everything comes right on the day all the hard work then seems worthwhile.

You can learn such a lot by watching the professionals: watch how they warm up their horses and work them in, what flatwork they use to supple them, how much they jump a horse before a class; watch the way they ride throughout and try to identify what it is in their technique that makes their riding effective. I have been lucky in that I was always able to watch my father jump right from when I was very young. It is important to have the right advice from the start; criticism is difficult for anyone to take, but it really is the only way to improve.

Inevitably every rider will adopt his own style, and some are far more individual than others – nor does style have to be orthodox to be effective. Annette Miller has an extremely distinctive way of riding – her weight tips forward onto her knees and her lower leg flips up in the air and she leaves the saddle completely when she jumps – but although this may not be the way the text books suggest you go about it she has certainly proved that she can get results! Both John and Michael Whitaker have styles of their own, being very calm and quiet riders, as do some of the riders from other countries; the Germans, for example, and in particular Franke Sloothaak, have developed a 'classical' seat. The more you watch, the more you will learn – and with a bit of luck, the more competitions you will win!

Affiliation and the Future

There are many 'newcomer' classes under BSJA
rules suitable for novice horses

# The BSJA

competing

The British Show Jumping Association initiates competitions which provide for horses of all standards, for those at the top of the ladder as well as for novices. Membership of the BSJA runs from 1 January to the end of December; therefore if you join in the summer, you still pay the full rate even though there are only six months left to run. Towards the end of the year (from about October onwards) there is a small discount for membership. There are various categories of membership and these can range from junior 'jumping' members to adult 'life' members. The rider has to register himself, as well as each horse that is going to compete in affiliated competitions – and it can be a very costly business if you have several horses to register. The current (1991) membership fee is around £50 for an adult member, and an additional £20 for a Grade B or C horse (Grade As, particularly those falling in the 'Top 100 Horses' slot, cost even more to register). There is also a membership facility for a non-jumping member; this really caters for the person who wishes to be kept up-to-date with BSJA news, and costs around £15. Junior membership is less expensive but, as with horses, a JA (Junior Grade A) pony will cost nearly twice as much to register as a JC/JD standard pony. As with everything, these fees are very likely to increase most years.

Further details about the BSJA can be obtained from: The British Show Jumping Association, British Equestrian Centre, Stoneleigh, Kenilworth, Warwickshire CV8 2LR. It is not necessary to be a member of the British Horse Society to be eligible for BSJA membership. Every BSJA member is issued with a very comprehensive rule book, which also gives detailed information concerning the different affiliated competitions. In addition to the rule book, you will also be sent a badge, and will receive the BSJA quarterly magazine *The Showjumper* which is entirely dedicated to news, results, reports, rule changes and so on in the showjumping discipline. The international circuit is far more involved; the rules are laid down by the FEI (Fédération Équestre Internationale) which is the governing body of the BSJA, and riders have to apply for a special licence under the FEI to compete in other countries. As one might expect, there is a fair amount of documentation involved.

Every horse is graded according to how much it has won in BSJA competitions, and its grade determines the affiliated competitions it is eligible for. So, when you register a horse with the BSJA, if it has not had any previous winnings in affiliated competitions then it starts at the bottom end of the scale as a Grade C; if it has, the grading system at the time of writing is as follows:

Horse	Winnings
Grade A	1,800 and over
Grade B	800 to 1,799
Grade C	0 to 799

Left: Competing with Boysie in the Dubai cup at Hickstead, in 1989

So what affiliated competitions does the BSJA provide? There is the British Novice Championship for Grade C horses or horses eligible to be registered for Grade C, not to have won £20 in either affiliated or unaffiliated competitions; successful riders then qualify for the Championship Final held at the Horse of the Year Show. Discovery and Newcomer competitions are open to Grade C horses and provide an inviting start to affiliated showjumping; the Pathfinders classes are also useful for novices because the two rounds to be jumped are not against the clock so riders aim for a double clear. The Foxhunter competitions are very popular and it is a great feeling if you can qualify for the final at Wembley. The rule book gives details as to the height and character of fences that will make up the courses for each type of competition. Competitions are run under 'Table A' or 'Table C', and these tables dictate a certain set of rules for a particular competition. Table A rules are categorised further into A1, A2, A3, A4 and A5 and each competition will state the category according to which it is being run.

Table A1: The first round is not against the clock. Those placed first equal qualify for the jump-off; the first jump-off is not against the clock, and those going clear go through to a second jump-off, which again is not timed. Those placed first equal divide the prize money.

Table A2: The first round is not against the clock and those placed first equal qualify for the first jump-off. The same applies for the first jump-off, but under Table A2 the second jump-off *is* against the clock. Competitors are placed on faults and time.

Table A3: The first round is not against the clock and those placed first equal qualify for the first jump-off. The first jump-off is against the clock and competitors are placed on faults and time.

Table A4: The first round is against the clock and competitors are placed on faults and time.

Table A5:

1 In competitions judged under Table A5 the course is divided into two sections. The first section is judged under Table A, not against the clock, but with a time allowed.

2 A competitor who incurs any jumping or time faults over the first section must leave the arena immediately on completion of the first section.

3 A competitor with a clear round over the first section must remain in the arena and must wait until the Judge rings the bell to indicate that he is ready for the competitor to start the second or jump-off section of the course. The competitor then jumps the jump-off section which is judged under Table A against the clock.

4 No penalties are incurred for falls or disobediences between the finish of the first section and the start of the jump-off section, but a competitor who fails to pass through the start of the jump-off section within 30 seconds of the bell incurs elimination.

5 In the event of equality of faults over the jump-off section of the course, time will decide. In the event of equality of faults and time over the jump-off section the prize money will be divided.

6 In the event of the number of competitors who reach the jump-off section of the course being sufficient to fill the prize list, the additional places will be decided on faults over the first section, prizes being divided as necessary.

7 The course for the jump-off section may include some of the obstacles forming part of the course for the first section and must include at least two additional obstacles which are to be built with greater heights and/or spreads than the first round obstacles.

8 Each section must be timed with automatic timing.

A Discovery competition ruling will probably be set out like this:

Discovery competition

1 Entry Qualifications: Horses in Grade C which have not won a total of £75 to be ridden by an Adult, Associate or Junior member.
2 Table A3
3 Speed 320m per minute
4 Course: 8 to 10 obstacles, heights and spreads will be as follows:

	Height	Spread
First two obstacles	0.90m	0.90m
One or two double combinations	0.90m	0.90m
Remaining obstacles	1.00m	1.00m

As the horses gain in experience and – we hope – ability, and accumulate more prize-money on their cards, they will upgrade to Grade B; the really good ones will ultimately become Grade A. However, although there are many Grade B horses jumping, very few of them will actually be able to cope with advanced courses even if they have won enough to be eligible for Grade A competition. There is a world of difference between Grade B and Grade A horses.

There is also a grading system for riders, known as the 'computer ranking lists', where riders accumulate points for being placed (one point for every £50 won in Grade A classes); the top horses are listed, and so are the leading owners, and as a result it all becomes a very competitive process, both to get on the list, or to stay on it – in fact the computer favours the rider with a string of Grade As who can get to a lot of shows. As things stand middle-ranked riders end up overjumping their horses to score more points, in order to qualify for, say, Olympia, and it can be a catastrophic régime for young horses.

All horses should have a break for six weeks or so sometime during the year. With the indoor winter jumping circuit, and indoor summer shows becoming increasingly a feature on the calendar, the jumping season indoors and outdoors is now all year round, and it is vital to work out the horse's programme so that it *does* include a rest period. Some horses jump better indoors, whereas others go better outside, so their holiday can be fitted in accordingly – if a horse is susceptible to the hard ground in the summer and suffers from jarring (particularly the case with older horses) it may be that indoor jumping is more suitable.

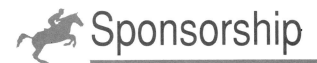

Sponsorship

To stay at the top of the grading systems riders have to ride, travel and compete full-time, so it is impossible to fit in any other job with a competitive career. The costs are enormous, and unless you are remarkably well off, then you will need a sponsor. The top riders spend a lot of time competing in other countries as well as in Britain, so there is a great deal of travelling involved, not to mention planning. Lesser ranked riders stay on the national circuit – and at grass roots level there are still many riders who are happy to compete at weekends as a hobby. This can only be a good thing if showjumping is still to be considered a sport.

So, you will need a sponsor to finance you. And as showjumping currently seems to be taking more of a back seat in the sports which are televised, it is now not the most attractive, or indeed viable, sport for companies to support: indeed, poor media coverage altogether means that company brand names are not being sufficiently exposed to make any significant impact. Sports programmes now show only the highlights of big competitions such as the Hickstead Derby meeting, the Horse of the Year Show, and Olympia, and this really is a great pity because there are so many followers of the sport who don't ride themselves but simply enjoy watching showjumping.

Why is it less attractive? People would probably say 'because it is not as entertaining

To get to the top of the ladder nowadays it is essential to have a good sponsor

as it used to be'; or 'the same people always win everything'. Again, why? and how might the situation be changed for the better? Maybe the qualifying rules for major shows and the computer ranking lists are to blame, whereby only the riders in the top twenty or thirty are invited to compete at the premier shows. Maybe Wembley has the right idea: it holds a qualifying event at South View for those *outside* the top thirty, from which another five go through to the Wembley final. And these should be allowed to jump in any Wembley classes, not just the afternoon ones – if they want to jump against Milton, let them! That would bring back a bit of entertainment! Olympia should do the same, and give a few 'borderliners' the chance to appear and jump at the Christmas Show. I bet if wouldn't be difficult to find a venue for another qualifier, either – everyone would fall over themselves to get the chance to qualify

for these shows, and any show organiser would be inundated with entries.

Rigid qualifying restrictions and the computer rankings mean that too many middle-ranked and young riders are being beaten by nothing but the system; it also means that that important ingredient of good sport isn't having a chance to come through – the underdog who comes good and beats the best. Look at Johnny Harris at the Royal International this year, and Geoff Billington who so *nearly* might have taken the Winner Takes All prize at the Horse of the Year Show. Give the public a chance to see new faces, some thrills and spills – that's what good sport is about! Top riders who always make it look too perfect and too easy risk being boring.

Racing seems to be the only horse sport with regular TV coverage: horse trials have minimum exposure, and as for the other equestrian disciplines, there is virtually nothing – only the occasional documentary. This is why sponsorship is so difficult to obtain, and why those of us who have got sponsors must make sure we help them as much as they help us. Brook Street sponsored me for several years and we operated a Brook Street Fan Club, so we were constantly trying to market both the Brook Street name and our own. My wife, Leanne, spent a great deal of time writing articles for the fan club magazine, and it was time well spent.

I think it is impossible for a rider to get to and, more importantly, stay at the top without a sponsor. It is not just finding an exceptionally good horse, or horses: it is financing their day-to-day keep, travelling to shows, entry fees, and all the other myriad expenses which makes showjumping such a costly business. Even riders at the top appreciate that it is impossible to predict even your likely winnings – a good horse may be laid off for a considerable period of time, or the rider may go through a bad patch. This sort of thing has happened to everybody, and then many riders will sell off young horses – and very often promising young horses that they would really like to keep themselves – in order to stay solvent. This is what we have to do, and why we have so many young horses coming in and out of our yard – there are more than a few that have to go for financial reasons rather than through choice. Furthermore there are many riders whose horses are sold by their owners: this is not the rider's decision because, ultimately, it is not the rider's horse. It is most disheartening to have an outstanding horse taken away from you; and it is even more depressing that many of our talented horses are all too often sold abroad.

 # Producing the young performance horse

Respected opinion holds that if we are not careful we will be left with only second-class horses, particularly as, unlike Germany and for example Holland and France, we do not have any sort of consistent breeding programme to ensure we get the best from our horses – it is all rather hit and miss, with mares and stallions not being bred particularly selectively, However, the inauguration of the High Performance Sales at Stoneleigh is a turn for the better: young horses are put forward by their breeder, the best are selected by a panel of experts, and then undergo two weeks training prior to the sale. This procedure contains all the signs that Britain is becoming more aware of producing 'the performance horse'; Germany has been staging performance sales along these lines for many years now, and it is well worthwhile observing their methods. Nonetheless, a system to promote the breeding of good competition horses will not help our sport if the horses it produces are consistently sold abroad.

Personally I feel that the mare contributes 75 per cent of the end product and the stallion 25 percent, so I would look for a Grade A mare and a fairly young, good jumping stallion. The main criterion must be to breed horses with a better-than-average chance of having a successful future as jumpers; with this in mind, several riders are jumping stallions in order to prove their worth as sires: for example Joe Turi and Vital; Graham Fletcher and Don Jones; the stallions John O'Gaunt and Henderson Didi jump regularly; Johnny Harris competes with Catherston Stud's Zandor. But again, any such breeding policy is pointless unless the structure of novice competitions is encouraging to young horses – and at the moment a four- or five-year old has to take on much older horses in Newcomer and Foxhunter classes; and the situation is made worse for the youngster because although the winnings limitations for these classes have been raised, prize-money has not. A horse can, therefore, be eligible for these classes for a long time, and to beat these older horses you have to go like hell against the clock – and with 20-odd clear rounds, what chance is there of winning on a four-year-old? In a Foxhunter you could be jumping against horses that are nearly Grade B. More serious, the easiest way to get through a huge entry is for the course builder to set awkward distances – and as we have seen, that is also the easiest way to ruin a young horse. But when people want to buy a young jumper, they want to see how much he has won – this is more important to them than the fact that he has jumped twenty or thirty clear rounds against strong opposition! So the point is, those of us producing young horses are not offered any reward for making a good job with four- and five-year-olds; and although a breeding programme is an excellent way to start producing jumpers, it must then be supported by a system which encourages the production of young jumpers, with a structured programme of suitable competitions for three-, four- and five-year-old horses.

Horses for Courses

Competing at the Royal International Horse Show
in 1991, with Silver Dust

competing

An experienced rider will be able to judge which courses suit a particular horse. Most of the top riders will do speed classes with one horse and Grand Prix type courses with another. Of course, not everybody has that many horses to choose from, in which case the rider needs to get the very best out of what he has got, even if this is only one horse. For example in a speed class or a jump-off, a slower horse may nonetheless be able to turn well, and time can be made up like this. Besides, some of the faster horses have a tendency to jump flat so a steady clear round could win the day. It is a case of assessing exactly what your horse can do best: and remember – never ask the impossible: it is quite pointless, and nine times out of ten is enough to put a horse off for life, particularly a youngster. Clover is a very good speed horse, whereas Silver Dust is not; however, he has the power to jump the biggest courses, so we usually save him for the bigger competitions – although he is very often not fast enough to take first place, he is usually careful enough to be in the ribbons. Again, I know where to push him and where to ease off, and so try to make up through good turns and clear rounds.

The following courses are of Grade A standard, but the basic principles of how to ride them stay the same, no matter how big or small the fences are. Let's take a look at three different courses, in fact ones that I jumped at the Horse of the Year Show in 1991.

The Taylor Woodrow Homes Speed Stakes

Fence number 1 is at the top end of the arena and it is essential to keep as close to the corner as possible on the approach. From 1 to 2 is a long gallop, so you really have to motor to 2. However, there is plenty of time to gain speed and then set up for 2 which is best taken at a slight angle (so you are virtually in a straight line with the arena exit) in preparation for fence 3 which involved a sharp left-hand turn. As I land over 2 I would turn immediately, looking all the time at fence 3 – so as we jump fence 2, my weight would be towards the inside indicating to the horse that I want him to turn straightaway, and so to land on the correct leg. I would be aiming to jump 3 at an angle, too (from the left-hand side of the wing to the right),

transferring my weight to the right-hand side and focussing on fence number 4. The triple bar at 4 needs a reasonable run to it, so I would really wind the horse up to get sufficient impulsion to clear this. You can really motor to the double at 5, taking a slight check on approach; it is a simple parallel, one stride, then pop out over the upright. It is about 21yd down to 6: in theory, this is four strides, but depending on the horse you are riding, it *is* possible to come down in three and save time. To set up for 7, I would be riding tight to the right wing of 6 to turn back for 7. So, over 7 we go, and a check before 8 so that I can turn inside the double to get back to 9. It is then a straightforward three strides (16yd) to 10 and a sharp left to 11 to finish.

Right: Competing at the Horse of the Year Show, 1988, on Boysie. Formerly ridden by David Bowen, Boysie was a very successful partner for Robert

COMPETITION *5. The Taylor Woodrow Homes* SHOW   HORSE OF THE YEAR SHOW 1991

Pro - Am.

		1st JUMP OFF		2nd JUMP OFF	
TABLE	*C.*	FENCES		FENCES	
SPEED	*350m.*	SPEED		SPEED	
DISTANCE		DISTANCE		DISTANCE	
TIME ALLOWED		TIME ALLOWED		TIME ALLOWED	
TIME LIMIT					

1·35.

COMPETITION *10 The Leading Show Jumper* SHOW   HORSE OF THE YEAR SHOW 1991

		1st JUMP OFF		2nd JUMP OFF	
TABLE	*A. Ar. 238 · 3 · B · M.S*	FENCES *3 A 4 6 8 9 10 A B 11*		FENCES	
SPEED	*325m*	SPEED	*325m*	SPEED	
DISTANCE	*490m.*	DISTANCE	*295m*	DISTANCE	
TIME ALLOWED	*90 Secs*	TIME ALLOWED	*55 Secs*	TIME ALLOWED	
TIME LIMIT	*180 "*				

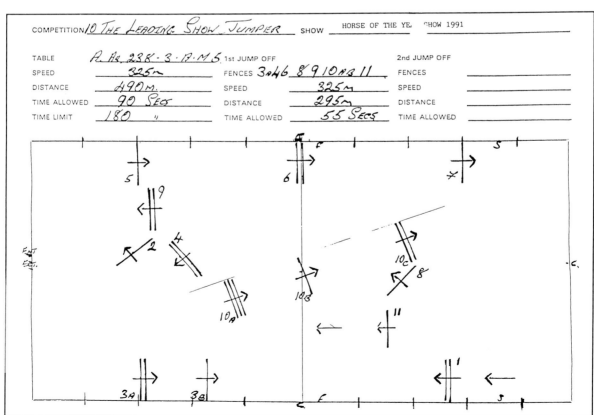

Leading Showjumper of the Year

Fence 1 is quite a tricky first fence, so a careful approach is needed right from the corner of the arena, on the correct leg lead. Then there is a long stretch down to 2 where I would push on a bit more so as not to accumulate time faults; it is an upright at 2, and so needs a fairly collected approach so that the horse will not jump flat. As we land from 2, I would be focussing on fence 3 which is a double. With firm pressure from my inside leg together with the reins I would hold the horse to the outside so that it gets as close to the arena barriers as possible in order to get a good approach to the double. This is a big oxer, one stride, and out over the vertical; I would be looking for a good stride on approach to the oxer. Again, it is essential to be aware of time: having jumped the double at 3, I would come inside number 11 to get back to 4. Once over 4, I would be making sure the horse was listening to me – any horse can get distracted as it passes the arena entrance and catches sight of people and other horses – and I would also be 'hugging' the arena boards as much as possible to keep in the corner and get a good approach for the vertical at 5.

Fences 5, 6 and 7 are in a line: in 1991 it was a vertical at 5, four strides to the oxer at 6 and four long strides to the planks at 7. I was riding Brookstreet Vanessa at the time, and it suited me to try and get another stride between 6 and 7; so I asked her to slightly stray from the line to put in this extra stride – this gave us time to get a really good stride for 7 which was a fence many riders were having down. This was one occasion when everything went right and my theory worked, as we cleared the fence without any problem.

Then it is a right-hand turn back to the vertical at 8 and a fairly long stretch to a big white parallel at 9 which, at the time, was catching many competitors out – horses find white difficult to focus on, in addition to which there was the distraction from the arena entrance. It would be very easy for a horse to make a mistake here. I jumped it to the left-hand side so that I could turn well to the treble at 10 and approach this in a good straight line: it is a triple bar, one stride to a vertical, two strides to an oxer, and a combination which is quite complicated because having jumped the triple bar, a horse would tend to jump rather flat over the vertical (which is 5ft 5in); so it is a case of the rider doing a sort of give, take, give to clear all three elements. Having jumped 10, then it is a right-hand turn and back over 11, which is a big vertical and one that cannot be galloped at!

The jump-off is over fences 3A, 4, 6, 8, 9, 10A and B and 11:
Start off on the left leg, as close to the arena boards as possible, and over 3A. It is a very tight turn to 4 if you try to go in between 10A and B, but it is possible and will save a lot of time – otherwise you go round the outside of 10B. At the time, I came between 10A and B and jumped fairly close to the left wing over 4, turning back sharp to fence 6. This is the sort of fence that you can probably chance and approach at more speed – I did at the time and got away with it. Then it is a tight turn back to 8 and a long gallop to 9 – again I chanced this one – turning back to the combination 10A and B. On landing from 10B I put my weight to the right-hand side in preparation for a sharp turn back to 11 and a strong gallop over the finish line.

In the *first round*, you can come in to fence 1 – an upright – from either the right or the left. If you approach it on the right leg you are on the correct lead for the parallel at 2 but there is not so much space to get a good approach for 1. Whereas if you come in on the left leg, although in theory it is the wrong lead, there is more room to approach the upright at 1 and change legs between 1 and 2 – this was the line I took at the time. The upright double at 3 needs a straight approach, and it is a sharp turn back from the boards (again, the horse must be listening to the rider, rather than looking out at the entrance). There is then plenty of time before the parallel at 4, and the horse can gain impulsion during this run-up. When I jumped this fence I thought I was going to end up in the Champagne Bar because it was a big jump close to the barriers!

You need to be close to the barriers to give yourself enough room to generate sufficient impulsion to clear the very wide triple bar at 5; then there is a long run down to the upright at 6 which stands at about 5ft 5in (a big fence made up entirely of poles). I would be wanting a fairly collected approach, but with sufficient energy to make the height and ensure the horse doesn't jump too flat and catch a pole. You will almost run into the arena boards after this fence, but keep a hold with the left rein, together with pressure from the inside leg, to stay in the corner for 7 which is a big parallel. It is three strides then over the upright at 8, and five strides to another big parallel at 9.

After 9 it is almost a U-turn back to the treble at 10, three parallels which require a fair amount of 'power from behind'. I would be looking for a good even stride to set the horse

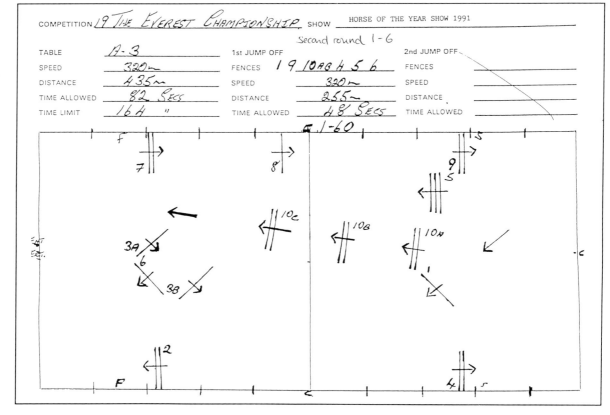

up well for all three elements. Remember about the spring that needs to be wound up and then released – this combination represents a particularly good example as we are looking for both height and width for all three fences.

Second Round (the jump-off): Fences 1, 9, 10A and B, 4, 5, and 6
Come into the first fence (1) at a slight angle (left to right) so that you have a good line to 9 between 10A and B. It is a very tight turn, and it may be that some will have to go round the outside of 10B to approach 9. During suspension over 9, the rider should be placing his weight to the inside in preparation for 10A and B. Then it is a sharp turn back to 4 and a good run to the triple bar at 5. Once over 5 it is another long run to the 5ft 8in upright (all poles) at 6, and it is easy for the horse to lose concentration here. It requires a really good jump, so care is needed – a good fence for spectator value but rather tension-building for us riders!

Silver Dust and I came fourth in this competition.

My Top Twelve Horse/Rider Partnerships

There are so many talented riders on the showjumping circuit that it was quite difficult to select the twelve horse/rider combinations that I rate most highly; however, the following partnerships have enjoyed outstanding success, where the style of riding and the type of horse really seem to click together. That a combination really *is* well suited must be the most important aspect of showjumping, otherwise neither party will get the results they deserve. You only have to watch the World Equestrian Games, where the very best riders in the world have to jump each other's horses during one of the phases; they can sometimes look complete novices (though admittedly horse and rider are not given much time to accustom themselves to each other). However, it is often a good example of how combinations sometimes click together.

Pierre Durand riding the incredible Jappeloup de Luze at Aachen in 1988.

Page 148: This combination does not really need identification...the amazing John Whitaker /Milton partnership

competing

46

John Whitaker – Milton (GB)

John is a very quiet rider; in fact you can hardly see him move, and in this lies the essence of the talented horseman. Moreover he stays very calm during competitions, an invaluable quality which succeeds not only in relaxing the horses he rides, but which means he can really think and concentrate on the course. Milton is probably the greatest horse of all time, and has the greatest number of supporters worldwide. He has fantastic balance, is extremely careful, and has more jump than any other horse I know.

What makes Milton special? Milton's sire, Marius, was a superb jumping stallion with wins which included the Queen Elizabeth II Cup in 1978 with the late Caroline Bradley. Milton went to Caroline when he was just six months old and it was apparent, even in his early days, that Milton had inherited much of the Marius magic. Milton's dam, Aston Answer qualified for the Foxhunter Championship at the Horse of the Year Show in 1983. Despite his breeding, I still feel that Milton is a 'one in a million' horse but Caroline's ability for training young horses was also quite exceptional so he did have a perfect start to life. The same sire/dam combination probably would not produce another Milton!

Quite apart from the aura that surrounds him as he enters the arena, he has a jumping style all his own, too, almost seeming to float over the jumps with his front legs at full stretch; in fact he clears the fences so well that this can cost him time against the clock. He is probably as near perfect as you can get in a showjumping horse, and the John/Milton partnership has done a great deal to popularise showjumping, certainly boosting ticket sales everywhere! Milton is almost beyond criticism; his only weakness is that he does not always like to go too deep to a vertical and can occasionally have a pole down.

Nick Skelton – St James (GB)

Nick is a real competitor in every sense of the word, and without doubt one of the best ring riders; he is always a good man for the big occasion, such as a prestigious Grand Prix competition. It is worth watching his technique and the way he thinks the course out, for he is a real quick-thinking rider – this shows particularly in his riding against the clock. St James was a very fast and agile jumper and they made a perfect combination. He did not lack scope in his jump and won a great many classes, and he would come out and do this every time, like Milton.

Michael Whitaker – Mon Santa (GB)

Michael is another great competitor and a very talented rider; he rides a great number of different horses and has the skill to achieve excellent results with all of them. He 'goes with' his horse always, almost daring it to do its job – an excellent rider to watch and learn from in the ring. Mon Santa, by Hard Study, is a true stamp of an Irish horse and has improved with age. He is a good horse to win the really big classes, and has jumped many double clear rounds in Nations Cups and Grands Prix – a very strong and powerful horse 'tailor-made' for showjumping.

Pierre Durand – Jappeloup (FR)

This was definitely a one man/one horse combination. Pierre produced the horse and probably did as well as any rider has ever done, including winning the individual gold at the Seoul Olympics. Jappeloup was certainly not an easy horse to ride and like all 'complicated' horses, Pierre had to be patient – any advance was made through trial and error. Having said that, Jappeloup was one of the most talented horses to have emerged in the last ten years, and I would go so far as to say that he was a better horse than Milton when he was at his peak. I am sure he would have won the World Equestrian Games had it not been for the phase where competitors ride each others' horses.

Paul Schockemöhle – Deister (GER)

Although Paul is probably not a rider with outstanding natural talent, he worked very hard to acquire skill, and achieved some incredible results. He is shrewd and thoughtful, and has ridden many talented horses; in fact his riding improved so dramatically that towards the end of his showjumping career he had become one of the most respected riders on the international scene. Deister was a very unorthodox horse. He could twist and turn anywhere, and showed great agility over fences. This did not always result in the most comfortable-looking of jumps, but he left the poles up and that is what showjumping is all about! A horse with a great deal of scope.

Eric Navet – Quito de Baussy (FR)
Another great horseman, French rider Eric Navet can ride most horses and is very much a man for the big one-off occasion, as he proved by winning the individual gold medal at the World Equestrian Games in Stockholm in 1990. Like John Whitaker, he is a very cool rider. Quito be Baussy is still a young horse and has a lot of scope and ability. He has a remarkably amenable character for a stallion and is basically a very careful jumper. I would say that he is a horse to jump to a finish rather than one that excels at speed.

Greg Best – Gem Twist (USA)
In the same way as Pierre Durand and Jappeloup, the USA's Greg Best has built up a finely tuned partnership with Gem Twist; he has proved his talent as a rider, and they have achieved great success together. Gem Twist is a blood horse with fantastic ability and demonstrates a catlike agility. A great partnership to watch – a superb quality horse.

Eddie Macken – Boomerang (IRE)
Eddie has a very good eye for a stride and a naturally good seat on a horse – whatever he rides, he looks equally good on them all; however, the one horse with which he enjoyed tremendous success was Boomerang. Personally, I think Boomerang has got to be one of the top three showjumping horses of all time, and it is a great pity that he was forced to finish his showjumping career so soon. Lameness got the better of him and he was finished at just twelve years old. By the Thoroughbred Battleburn and out of a hunter mare, Boomerang was another crowd-puller; he was also probably one of the best-ever Grand Prix winners.

Gert Wiltfang – Roman (GER)
On his day Gert Wiltfang was virtually unbeatable, but the strange thing about him was that he would be here one day and gone the next. He would win five out of seven big competitions, and then would not be seen or heard of at all for another three months! Gert was a very accurate and physical rider, and Roman was a great big German jumping horse; he was only with Gert for 18 months but the success they enjoyed during that space of time was quite remarkable.

Liz Edgar – Everest Forever (GB)
Liz is probably the best rider of all time. She is a thinking rider through and through, and her opinion is widely respected throughout the showjumping fraternity. She is extremely accurate and very fast – a real winner, and always knows exactly what she is doing. Forever is a great horse and together they won many classes over many years.

David Broome – Philco (GB)
A great all-round rider and a man who knows how to get the best out of a good horse; David has a superb sense of timing. To watch him in a jump-off his speed is deceptive – he gets from A to B very quickly but without seeming to hurry. Philco, an ex-racehorse and quality Thoroughbred, really suited David's way of riding; his assets included his aptitude for carefulness – a truly honest character and one of the old-fashioned Grade A type horses.

Harvey Smith – Salvador (GB)
This is a rider I know fairly well and one I could not miss out! Harvey can ride any horse and win any competition – he is a great man for winning classes on horses that are not always good enough to win them. He is what I would describe as a true 'blood and guts' rider – a real physical rider who gives it his all. He has to be the fastest of anybody against the clock. Salvador was a problem type of horse but had a huge jump. Basically he was very careful and demonstrated a good jumping technique – there was no course too big for him. However, only somebody like my father could ride him.

Index

i
n
d
e
x

152